The Official Guide to

Family Tree Maker 2005.

The Official Guide to

Family Tree Maker 2005

Esther Yu Sumner

MyFamily.com

Library of Congress Cataloging-in-Publication Data

Sumner, Esther Yu.
   The official guide to Family tree maker 2005 / by Esther Yu Sumner.
      p. cm.
   Includes index.
   ISBN 1-59331-270-9 (pbk. : alk. paper)
   1. Family tree maker. 2. Genealogy—Computer programs. 3. Genealogy—Data
processing. I. Title.
   CS14.S86 2004
   929'.1'0285—dc22

                                                                    2004021678

Published by MyFamily.com, Inc.

P.O. Box 990

Orem, UT 84059

10 9 8 7 6 5 4 3 2

Printed in the United States of America

Table of Contents

Acknowledgments

Thank you to Christine Connor and Matt Wright, who provided much needed input while I wrote this book. Christine provided invaluable technical feedback during the organization and writing. As my editor, Matt polished the final product, from overall structure down to minute words and punctuation. This book would not be the work you see today were it not for their input. Also, thank you Jennifer Utley, Director of Publishing at MyFamily.com for her direction and guidance and Robert Davis for his patience and input while designing this book. Thank you also to Rhonda R. McClure, who wrote the last four versions of the Family Tree Maker guidebook, and provided inspiration for this edition. I would also like to acknowledge Jodi Moore, who assisted with image collections, and Myra Vanderpool Gormley and Julie Duncan for providing technical edits. And finally, thank you to my husband John, for his support and patience while I worked on this book.

Introduction

This guidebook will help you learn Family Tree Maker 2005 quickly, leaving you more time to research your family history. You will learn many of the convenient features a casual Family Tree Maker user never discovers, resulting in more efficient data entry and navigation, and more ways to enhance your research visually to share with others. Even if you have never used a genealogy program before, you will find that Family Tree Maker's interface and options make it possible to keep track of even the most tangled of family trees. This book introduces you to many of the features available in Family Tree Maker so you can enjoy your research.

Who Should Read This Book?

This book is written with the novice computer user in mind. You are taken on a hands-on trip through the Family Tree Maker program. The many illustrations let you check your progress as you master each new feature or process. Even if you are familiar with computers, though, you may have only recently been introduced to Family Tree Maker, or simply want to know what great features you have not yet discovered in the program. This book offers you an easy-to-follow tour of the program and all that you can accomplish. As you compare your own screen to the screen images in the book you will be able to see if you are using the program correctly.

This book is organized by tasks. Some tasks may require many steps, and others may branch off into enhancements or additional features. A quick perusal of the Table of Contents should lead you right to the process you are trying to accomplish, or check the index in the back of the book.

Special Features of This Book

As you work with this book, you will accomplish many tasks. This is by design, so that you can master what you need in an easy-to-follow format. There are a couple of features, though, that will supply you with additional information as you work with the Family Tree Maker program.

Tips offer you useful hints about features in Family Tree Maker that can speed up the task at hand or enhance your report output.

Notes offer additional information about Family Tree Maker or about genealogy and sharing your family tree.

In the appendixes you will find help for installing the Family Tree Maker software and useful tables of keyboard shortcuts to make your data entry speedier.

Good luck, and have fun.

PART I

Introduction to Family Tree Maker

Getting Started with Family Tree Maker

Before you take advantage of the many features of Family Tree Maker 2005, you must know how to launch or open it. Be sure you have some of your family history information ready to enter so that you can begin to see how the program handles your family data. Family Tree Maker offers different methods for opening the program and beginning a new Family File. In this chapter, you will learn how to:

- Start Family Tree Maker from the menu or desktop
- Create a new Family File or open an existing Family File
- Enter basic information in Family View
- Exit Family Tree Maker

Get started with Family Tree Maker by learning how to launch the program, and by creating your family file. If you do not understand the meaning of a term used in Family Tree Maker, check the glossary in the back of the book, which addresses technical computer terms (click, dialog box, icon, etc.), Family Tree Maker terms (Edit Individual dialog box, Family View, etc.), and genealogy words (GEDCOM, Ahnentafel, etc.)

Starting Family Tree Maker 2005

When Family Tree Maker was installed (see Appendix A, "Installing Family Tree Maker") the installation set up two different ways for you to launch the program.

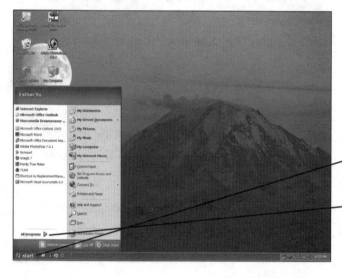

Launching Family Tree Maker from the Menu

For each program installed on your computer, there is a Start Menu option that allows you to launch the program. Family Tree Maker is no different.

1. Click **Start** on the Windows taskbar. The Start menu will appear.

2. Select **Programs** (or **All Programs** in Windows XP). The Programs menu will appear.

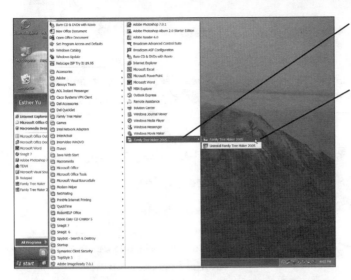

3. Select **Family Tree Maker 2005** from the Programs menu. The Family Tree Maker menu will appear.

4. Click **Family Tree Maker 2005** from the Family Tree Maker 2005 menu. Family Tree Maker will start.

Launching Family Tree Maker from the Desktop

When you install Family Tree Maker on your computer, the program leaves an application icon on the Windows desktop. This launches the Family Tree Maker program, so you do not have to use the Start menu every time.

1. Double-click on the **Family Tree Maker 2005 icon on the desktop.** Family Tree Maker will start.

The Welcome Screen

If this is your first time using Family Tree Maker 2005 on this computer, Family Tree Maker will greet you with a one-time Welcome Screen. The Welcome Screen will allow you to view a Getting Started tutorial if you have an Internet connection, as well as to choose whether you want to create a new file or open an existing file from a previous version of FTM, or from Ancestry Family Tree, or a GEDCOM (GEnealogical Data COMmunications format).

WHAT IS A GEDCOM?

GEDCOM is a file format that allows you to share genealogical data with others, even if they are using a different genealogy program. Family Tree Maker can import and export GEDCOMs. Learn more about sharing Family Files and GEDCOMs in Chapter 15.

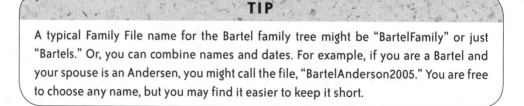

The Welcome Screen Has Three Options:

- Click **Show Me** to complete a tutorial. You can also complete the tutorial at a later time by selecting **Getting Started Tutorial** from the **Help** menu.

- Click **Create New** if you are a new user, and to begin using Family Tree Maker with your first Family File.

- Click **Open Existing** if you already have a Family File or GEDCOM.

Creating a New Family File

Click **Create New** from the Welcome Screen. If Family Tree Maker opened but skipped the welcome screen (which indicates you have opened this program previously), click **File** from the menu bar. A drop-down menu will appear. Click **New**. The New Family File dialog box will open.

TIP

A typical Family File name for the Bartel family tree might be "BartelFamily" or just "Bartels." Or, you can combine names and dates. For example, if you are a Bartel and your spouse is an Andersen, you might call the file, "BartelAnderson2005." You are free to choose any name, but you may find it easier to keep it short.

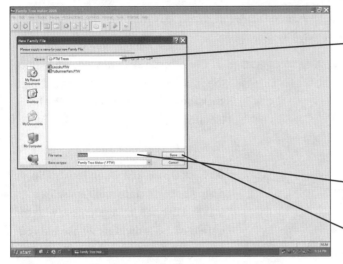

To name the Family File:

1. Click the **Save in** drop-down arrow in the New Family File dialog box, and click where you want to save your file, or allow Family Tree Maker to save to the default location, which is in your My Documents folder, in a folder called FTW.

2. Type the name you have chosen into the **File name** field.

3. Click **Save**. Family Tree Maker automatically defaults to the "Family Tree Maker (*.FTW)" file format. The New Family File dialog box will close and Family Tree Maker will open to Family View. You are ready to begin adding information to your Family File.

NOTE

Family Tree Maker will automatically open the last file you were working in when you launch the program, but it's a good idea to make a note of where you have saved your file in case you need to locate the file later.

TIP

The **Save as type** section (below **File name**) allows you to choose a file format, but Family Tree Maker defaults to the correct file format, .FTW.

Opening an Existing Family File

You may already have a Family File or GEDCOM you want to open in Family Tree Maker. If you did not click **Open Existing** from the Welcome Screen, you can still open the file.

1. Click **File** to open the File menu (Family Tree Maker menus are described at the beginning of Chapter 2).

2. Click **Open** in the File menu. The Open Family File dialog box will open. The dialog box functions similarly to the New Family File dialog box.

3. Click the **Look in** drop-down to find the folder where the file is located, then click the folder when you find the file location.

4. Click to select the file.

5. Click **Open**. The Open Family File dialog box will close and Family Tree Maker will open to Family View with the details of the individual whose file you opened. You are ready to continue adding information to your Family File.

As you enter information in your Family File, Family Tree Maker will automatically save the details as you go.

TIP

If you clicked **Create New** from the Welcome Screen, you were taken to the New Family File dialog box. At this point, you can still open an existing file by clicking the **Open File** button at the bottom of this dialog box to go to the Open Family File dialog box.

Entering Names

Family Tree Maker automatically defaults to the Family View page, where you will see a view representing three generations of a family. In this chapter, you will fill in very basic information for the two primary individuals in Family View – **Husband** and **Wife**. You will learn how to use Family View in greater detail in Chapter 3.

TIP

A common practice in family history record-keeping is to start with what you know best – basic details about yourself, your children, and your parents – and then to work backwards to ancestors.

Entering Information about Husband or Wife

These instructions are for the Husband fields, but also apply to the Wife fields. Make sure you are still in Family View.

1. Click in the **name** field in the Husband box, and type the person's name (first name, middle name, last name).

> **NOTE**
>
> You can change the setting from Husband to a different title (e.g., Father, Spouse) by changing the Preference under the **File** menu (see Chapter 16). When recording names for women, use maiden names only. (You may choose to display their married names in reports and charts if you wish.)

2. Press the **tab** key to go to the next field. Type the birth date in the **Birth date** field.

> **TIP**
>
> In addition to using **tab** keys, you can move from one field to the next by pressing the **enter** key or by clicking in the field.

Understanding Names in Family Tree Maker

Generally, when entering the name of an ancestor in Family Tree Maker, you will simply type the name (as it appears in the record or resource you are viewing) directly into the **Name** field in Family Tree Maker's Family View page. However, there are a few instances where the surname (last name) is not just a single word. In such instances, you will need to identify the surname for Family Tree Maker with backward slashes (\). There are many different reasons that a surname may be more than one word. This is especially true in the research of European names. Here are some examples, with the backward slash mark included:

George \de la Vergne\ 　　　　　 Peter \Van Der Voort\

Pierre \Bourbeau dit Lacourse\ 　　 Teresa \Garcia Ramirez\

Another instance in which you might need to use backward slashes is when entering someone who does not have a last name, such as a person of Native American descent. For instance, your ancestor might have been known as Running Bear. This name would be entered in Family Tree Maker as Running Bear\\.

A common practice in genealogy is to write the entire last name for each individual in capital letters. This makes it easier to distinguish names in documents. For example, Arah Shumway would be written Arah SHUMWAY. If you use the capitalized last name, you will probably want to make sure the Family Tree Maker spell checker does not search for capitalized words. You can do this in the Preferences dialog box discussed in Chapter 16.

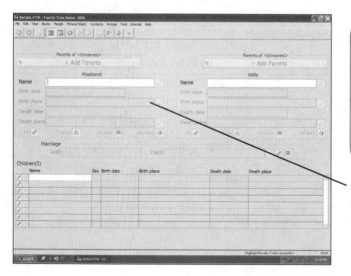

NOTE

The date will be displayed in the standard format used by most genealogists: day month year. You may change how this is displayed in the Preferences dialog box discussed in Chapter 16.

3. Press the **tab** key to go to the next field, and type the individual's birth location in the **Birth Place** field.

TIP

Family Tree Maker has a special feature called Fastfields, through which the software remembers locations you have typed previously. You may notice the program automatically finishing the name of a location for you as you begin to type it, because it "remembers" the word. If the fastfield offers an incorrect suggestion, you can continue typing over the location. You can also click on the trash can button that appears when Fastfields is activated, to make Family Tree Maker forget that particular Fastfield term.

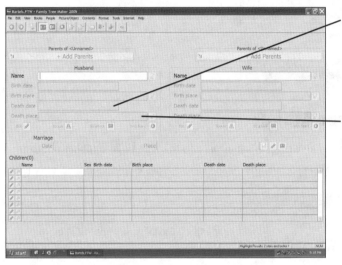

4. Press the **tab** key to go to the next field, and type a date in the **Death Date** field. If the individual is living or you do not know the death date, simply skip over this field and the next.

5. Press the **tab** key to go to the next field, and type the place of death in the **Death Place** field.

NOTE

You must first enter information in the name field before Family Tree Maker will allow you to enter other information about an individual. However, you can enter a question mark and then replace the question mark with a name later.

6. Click in the **Name** field for the Wife and complete each field the same way you completed the Husband fields.

Exiting Family Tree Maker

You have now seen the basics of entering information into the Family Tree Maker program. When you have finished your session, you will want to close the program.

1. Click **File**. The file menu will appear.

2. Click **Exit**. Family Tree Maker will close.

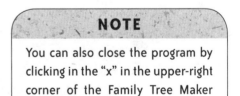

NOTE

You can also close the program by clicking in the "x" in the upper-right corner of the Family Tree Maker window.

Learning General Family Tree Maker Features

Learning any software program requires an introduction to its interface. There are usually some new menu items, toolbar buttons, and choices that are specific to the program. This is certainly true of Family Tree Maker, and this chapter introduces you to those items. In this chapter, you will learn how to:

- Use the menu and toolbars
- Use dialog boxes and scroll bars
- Display views, charts, and reports

Using the Menus and Toolbars

As you look at the top of your Family Tree Maker screen, you will see a number of small illustrations and words. These are the toolbar buttons and menus, which were referenced in Chapter 1. This section introduces you to these features.

By now you should have entered a Husband and Wife in Family View or filled in the information by opening an existing file or importing a GEDCOM. If you have not done so, please go back to Chapter 1 and follow those steps. Many of the menu and toolbar items discussed in this chapter will not be activated until you begin entering family information.

Using Menus

Menus are lists of the functions built into software programs. As in most software programs, the Family Tree Maker menus are activated by clicking on the words that appear along the top bar of the Family Tree Maker program window. Each menu contains a list of related commands that will appear in a drop-down menu.

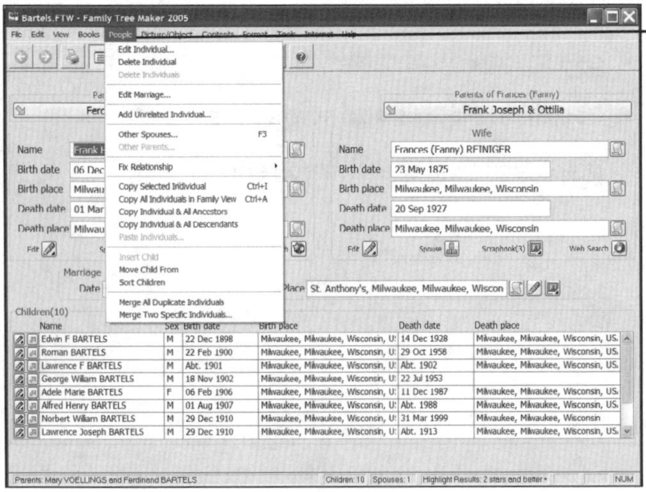

1. Click on the **People** menu in Family Tree Maker. A drop-down menu will appear below the menu name.

> **NOTE**
>
> In Family Tree Maker, like in many software applications, options that are not available are grayed out.

2. Select **Fix Relationship** from the **People** menu. A fly-out menu will appear. Note that you only had to select Fix Relationship, not click on it, in order for the fly-out menu to appear. If you planned to perform a function from this fly-out menu, you would simply click on an item from the fly-out menu.

Keyboard Shortcuts

Menu commands have keyboard shortcuts. You can use these shortcuts to execute commands, rather than using the menus.

a. Press **ALT** to view the shortcuts. Each menu item now has one letter underlined. If all your menu items are grayed out, you may not have entered enough information yet, or you may need to click to select an item first. You may also need to close a dialog box.

b. Press **ALT** plus the underlined letter of the menu that you want to open. For example, after you press the **ALT** key, the V is underlined in View. Press **V**. This will open the View menu. Notice that each menu item in the View menu also has one underlined letter.

c. Press one of the underlined letters in the menu. For example, press **F**. The Family View will open. Now you know that **ALT, V, F** in succession will open Family View in Family Tree Maker.

Using Toolbars

There is one main toolbar in Family Tree Maker. Family Tree Maker also has a vertical tool-bar for charts and reports, which will be covered in Chapter 8. The toolbar offers buttons to access some of the more popular win-dows, as well as a few shortcut buttons to some of the unique commands.

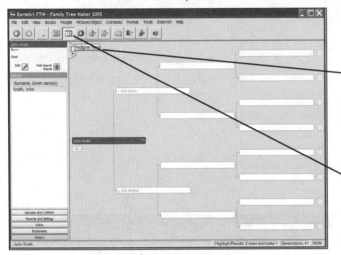

1. Place your mouse pointer over the **toolbar** buttons. The name of the func-tion of that toolbar button will appear in bubble help (a small pop-up window).

2. Click on the **Pedigree View** button on the toolbar. The Pedigree View win-dow will appear.

Understanding Dialog Boxes and Scroll Bars

Dialog boxes are small windows that appear in front of your Family Tree Maker screen that require an action. Each dialog box has a different purpose, but generally, dialog boxes contain command buttons and various options to help you carry out a command or task. You had to view a dialog box before you could begin entering information in Family Tree Maker, either an Open Family File dialog box or a New Family File dialog box. Try this example to view another of many dialog boxes used in Family Tree Maker.

1. Click the **Family View** button to return to Family View.

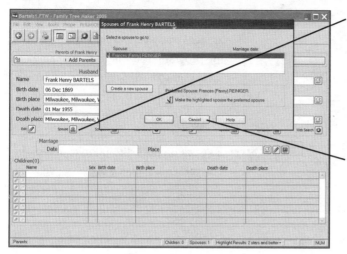

2. Click the **Spouse** button below the Husband's Death place field. The **Spouses of** dialog box will open. This is an example of a dialog box that allows you to add additional spouses (e.g., a widower re-marrying) to an individual or view other spouses (e.g., an ex-wife).

3. Click the **Cancel** button to close the dialog box without making any changes.

Displaying the Different Views, Charts, and Reports

Family Tree Maker offers a variety of views, charts, and reports to display your family data. Some displays focus on a single-family unit, while others are multi-generational, including ancestors and descendants. This section is a quick overview of each of these features in Family Tree Maker and how to access the features. You will learn more details on how to use each view, chart, and report in the following chapters.

Exploring Family View and Associated Features

The Family View is the screen in which you entered information about a husband and wife in Chapter 1. Family Tree Maker opens to this view each time you re-open your program. This is the easiest and most logical place for you to enter basic information about each individual. This view represents three generations of a family group – a primary couple, the couple's children and the couple's parents, and includes easy buttons to click to relevant functions.

1. Click on the **Family View** button to access Family View from anywhere in the program. You will go to the Family View of the individual you last selected. Chapter 3 will go in-depth on how to use the features on the page.

2. Click on the **Edit** button to access the Edit Individual dialog box.

The Edit Individual dialog box can be accessed from several places: Family View, Pedigree View, and from several reports and charts. This dialog box allows you to enter and view any details about a person other than relationship information.

3. Click on the **Edit** button for Marriages to access the Edit Marriage dialog box.

The Edit Marriage dialog box is similar to the Edit Individual dialog box, but focuses on the details about the relationship between the couple rather than an individual. Click **Cancel**, **OK**, or the **x** in the upper right-hand corner to close the window.

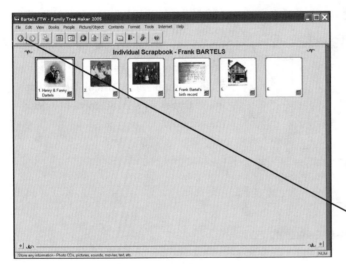

4. Click on one of the **Scrapbook** buttons.

There is a scrapbook for each individual and each marriage. This page organizes any images or other multimedia objects you may want to associate with an individual or marriage. (Your Scrapbook page will likely be empty because unlike this example, you have probably have not saved any pictures to your scrapbook yet.)

5. Click on the **back arrow** button. You will return to the last page you were on before you went to the Scrapbook page.

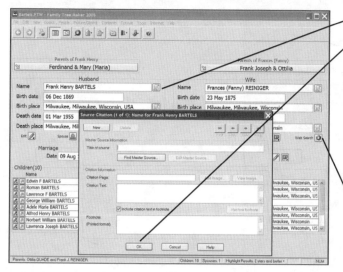

6. Click on one of the **Source** buttons.

7. The Source-Citation dialog box will open. This page allows you to record details about where information was found and is especially useful when comparing conflicting information. Click **Cancel**, **OK**, or the **x** in the upper right-hand corner to close the window.

8. Click on one of the **Web Search** buttons.

9. If you are connected to the Internet, the Web Search report will open for the individual whose Web Search button you clicked. You'll be able to view search results for additional records about this individual, as well as merge findings into your Family File. Click on the **back arrow**.

10. Click on one of the **Parent** buttons.

You will be taken to the Family View page of the parents on whose name you clicked. The individual from whom you navigated will be listed in the Children field. If you have not entered information about the parent yet, the Husband and Wife fields will be blank.

11. Click on the **Navigate** button next to the child. You will be taken back to that child's Family View page, with the child listed as the Husband or Wife.

NOTE

The parent and child navigating buttons provide one easy way to move to different Family View pages. You will learn additional ways to navigate to individuals, including the Index of Individuals, in later chapters.

Exploring Pedigree View

The Pedigree View is the second major work area in Family Tree Maker, and provides a more comprehensive view of your Family File. The Pedigree View allows you to see several generations at once and provides an easy way to navigate through each member of your family tree.

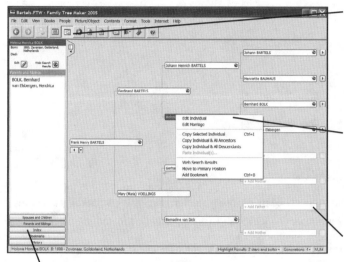

1. Click on the **Pedigree View** button. The person you last selected in the Family View will appear in the primary or root position of the pedigree tree, and the ancestors will branch to the right.

2. Right-click on a name in the chart. A drop-down menu will appear with additional functions you can perform for that individual, e.g., Edit individual, Move to Primary Position.

3. Click on the node labeled **+Add Father** or **+Add Mother.** An Edit Individual dialog box will appear. This option will not be available if every node in your current Pedigree View already has a name entered. Close the dialog box by clicking **Cancel**.

4. The Side Panel on the left side of the screen will help you jump to the Pedigree Views of other individuals. It also provides more information about whichever individual in the tree is selected. The details at the top of the Pedigree View Side Panel stay the same, while the main section of the Side Panel changes according to which button you click: **Details, Spouses and Children, Parents and Siblings, Index, Bookmarks**, and **History**. The Index section should by default be expanded. If it is not, click on **Index** to see how the Index section appears.

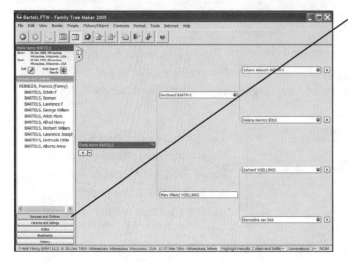

5. Click on the **Spouses and Children** button. The Spouses and Children section will expand and the Index section will collapse. As you click on each button in the Side Panel, the section will expand and the one before it will collapse.

Exploring Tree Charts

Family Tree Maker offers a wide variety of printable tree charts so you can quickly view the relationships between family members in various visually appealing formats.

If you only have a couple of individuals in your tree, some of these charts will be very small, sometimes containing only one name. In addition, some of sample charts shown below have already been customized with special borders, images, etc., which you will learn to do in Chapter 8.

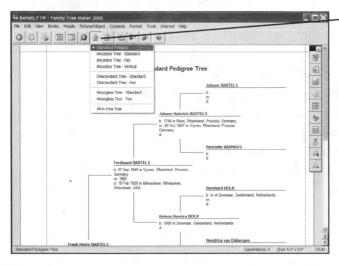

1. Click the **charts** button from the toolbar. A drop-down list will appear listing several chart options.

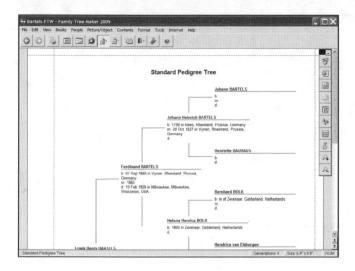

2. Click on **Standard Pedigree**. The Standard Pedigree Tree will appear.

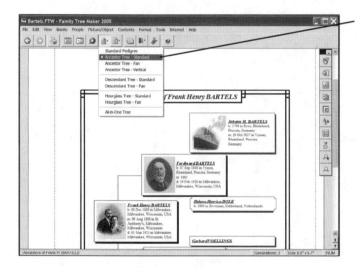

3. Click the **charts** button from the toolbar. Click **Ancestor Tree - Standard** from the list. The Ancestor Tree – Standard will appear.

4. Click the **charts** button from the toolbar. Now try clicking some of the other charts available – the following diagrams show examples of each type of chart.

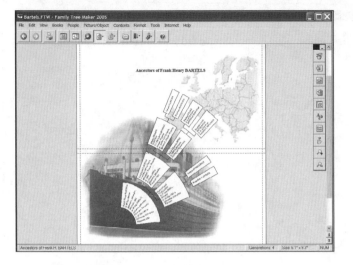

Ancestor Tree – Fan (with a New World Template in the background)

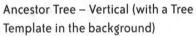

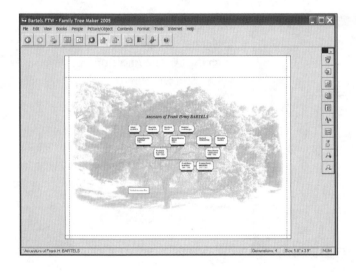

Ancestor Tree – Vertical (with a Tree Template in the background)

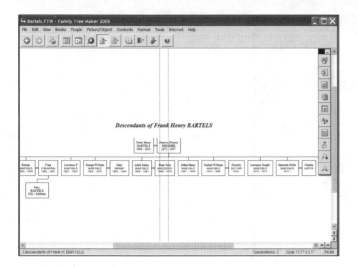

Descendant Tree – Standard (with dotted lines showing how a larger chart would print on multiple sheets of 8 ½ x 11 paper)

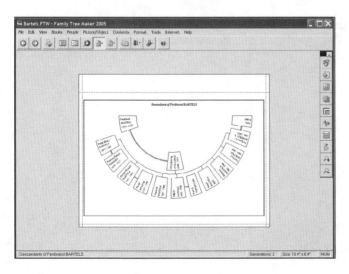

Descendant Tree – Fan

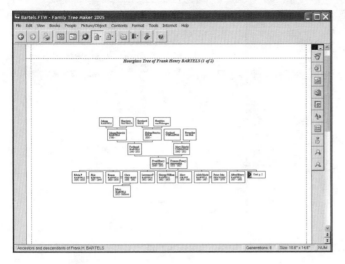

Hourglass Tree – Standard

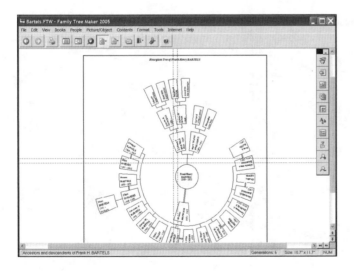

Hourglass Tree – Fan

All-in-One Tree

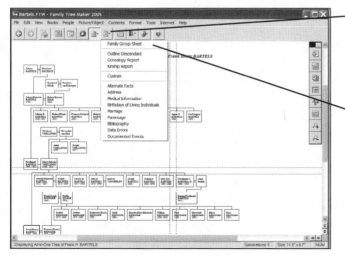

Exploring Reports

Family Tree Maker offers a wide variety of reports to view or print. You can also create your own custom report.

Most of the reports you view at this point will have few details listed if you have not yet entered more than a couple names in Family View. Chapter 3 thoroughly covers entering more details about your family.

1. Click the **reports** button from the toolbar. A drop-down list will appear listing several report options.

2. Click on **Family Group Sheet**. The Family Group Sheet is one of the most commonly used reports by family historians. Like Family Tree Maker's Family View, it includes information on three generations of a family.

3. Click the **reports** button from the toolbar.

4. Click on **Genealogy Report**.

5. Click the **reports** button from the toolbar. Now try clicking some of the other reports available. The Custom Report allows you to choose the content as well as the formatting. For more detailed instructions on creating custom reports, see Chapter 9.

PART II

Building Your Tree and Navigating in Family Tree Maker

3

Entering Information About a Family in Family View

Much of your time in Family Tree Maker will be spent entering the data you have uncovered about your family. At first, this information will likely focus on your small family group: yourself, your parents, and your children. As you continue, your focus will likely turn to your ancestral lines and other family groups: your parents, your grandparents, and your great-grandparents, for instance. Family Tree Maker helps you stay organized as you begin to enter information in Family View. In this chapter, you'll learn how to:

- Enter individuals and events
- Change the date format
- Add additional spouses, parents, and children
- View other family groups
- Enter in-depth individual facts in the Edit Individual dialog box
- Enter in-depth marriage facts in the Edit Marriage dialog box

Begin Your Family File Using Family View

In Chapter 1, you were introduced to the basics of entering information. This chapter covers how you enter information in Family View, including adding individuals, events, and related details. Before you start this tutorial, make sure you are in Family View.

Entering Information about Individuals

You likely completed step 1 and 2 in Chapter 1, but these steps will be quickly reviewed again.

1. Click in the **Name** field in the Husband box. Type the husband's first name, middle name, last name.

2. Click in the **Name** field for Wife. Type the wife's first name, middle name, maiden name. Always use maiden names for females. You can choose to display married names in charts and reports if you wish.

TIP

Enter the last name in all-capital letters so you can distinguish first and middle names from last names at a glance, e.g., Frances Louise REINIGER. You will also be able to enter nicknames, married names, etc., in the Edit Individual dialog box, which will be addressed later in this chapter.

3. Click in the first row in the **Children** box, under the **Name** column. Enter the child's name.

TIP

When entering children in Family View, Family Tree Maker will assume the child has the same surname as the father and add the surname automatically. You can ignore the suggested last name by continuing to type over the Fastfield.

Entering Events

The method for entering events is similar for husband, wife, and children, even though the fields for children may look a bit different from the fields for husband and wife.

1. Click in the **Birth date** field. Enter the birth date.

2. Press the **tab** key. The cursor will move to the next field. Type a location in the **Birth place** field.

3. Press the **tab** key. The cursor will move to the next field. Type a date in the **Death date** field.

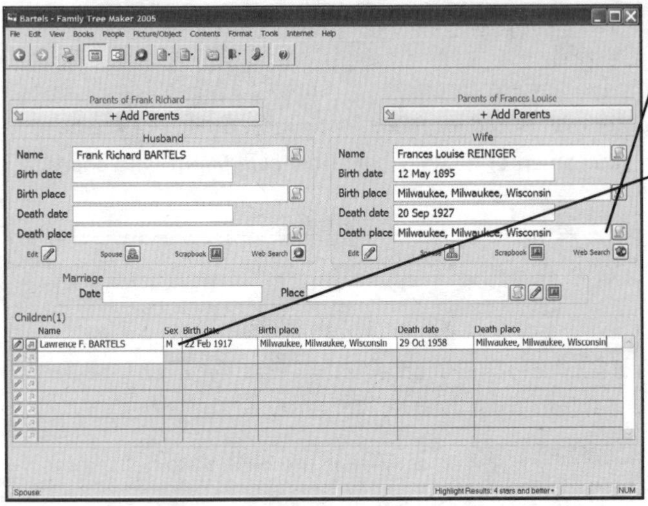

4. Press the **tab** key. The cursor will move to the next field. Type a location in the **Death place** field.

5. In the **Sex** field, list the child's gender, using "F" for Female, "M" for Male, or a "?" if unknown. Family Tree Maker assumes the Husband is male and Wife is female. (You can later move the Husband or Wife to the child position of Family View, and change the gender status.)

NOTE

You can add as many children as you like, by pressing the tab key at the end of each row to start a new entry. If you enter more than eight children, a scroll bar will appear on the right side of the Children box, which you can use to navigate to any children not visible on the screen. You can always check the parentheses in the "Children ( )" heading to see how many children are currently listed.

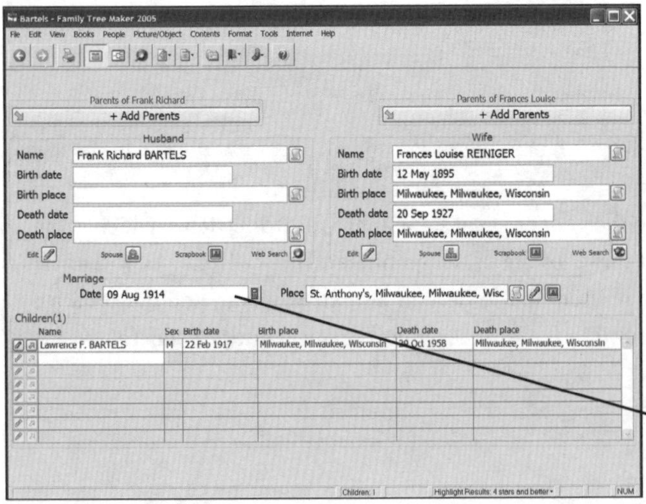

Entering Marriage Information

Family View displays the date and location of the main couple's marriage. You will learn how to view and add additional information about marriages later in this chapter (see Adding Details About a Marriage).

To enter a marriage date and place:

1. Click in the Marriage **Date** field. Type the date.

2. Press the **tab** key to move to the next field. Type the marriage location in the Marriage **Place** field.

Changing the Date Format

If you do not like the format in which Family Tree Maker shows dates, you can change the default setting.

1. Click on **File** in the menu bar. The File menu will appear.

2. Click on **Preferences** in the File menu. The Preferences dialog box will open.

3. Click the **Dates** tab in the Preferences dialog box. The Dates tab will open.

4. Click the **DMY** radio button to show dates by day-month-year or click the **MDY** radio button to show dates by month-day-year.

5. Click the **Styles** drop-down list and click the month style.

6. Click **OK**. The Dates dialog box will close, and the selections will automatically take effect in the Family Tree Maker program.

Adding Additional Spouse and Parents

The Family View screen allows only one spouse to be displayed at a time. However, there are times when a researcher needs to enter more than one spouse for an individual, for example if a widower remarries. Family Tree Maker allows you to add multiple spouses.

1. Click the **Spouse** button in **Family View**, next to the individual who has another spouse. The Spouses dialog box will open.

2. Click the **Create a new spouse** button. A message box will appear, asking if you want the new spouse to be associated with the children previously entered for an individual.

3. Click **Yes** if you want to create an association or **No** if you do not. You will be able to indicate the relationship between the child and each parent (e.g., step-parent, adopted, natural, etc.) in step 13. You will be taken to a new Family View page with blank fields for the new spouse.

4. Fill in the blank fields about the spouse.

5. Enter the information you know about the marriage event. The marriage event fields will be gray until you add the name of the spouse.

Preferred Spouse

If you enter more than one spouse, you need to indicate a "preferred" spouse. The preferred spouse is the spouse that the Family View, Pedigree View, charts, and reports will default to displaying. Usually, the logical selection is the spouse that had children in your family line.

6. Click on the **Spouse(s)** button in Family View. The Spouses dialog box will open.

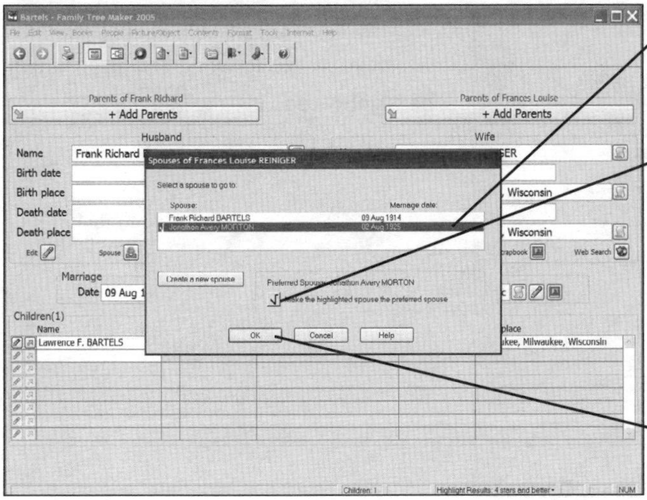

7. Click on the spouse you want to appear as the preferred spouse. The spouse will be highlighted.

8. Click on the **checkmark** button next to **Make the highlighted spouse the preferred spouse**. The checkmark will appear on the left of the selected individual, in the Spouse column above, to indicate the individual is the preferred spouse.

9. Click on **OK**. The Spouses dialog box will close.

Viewing a Different Spouse

You can only view the information and children of one spouse at a time, so you may need to switch spouses when you want to work with a specific family. You will also need to change spouses if you want to add information about that particular marriage.

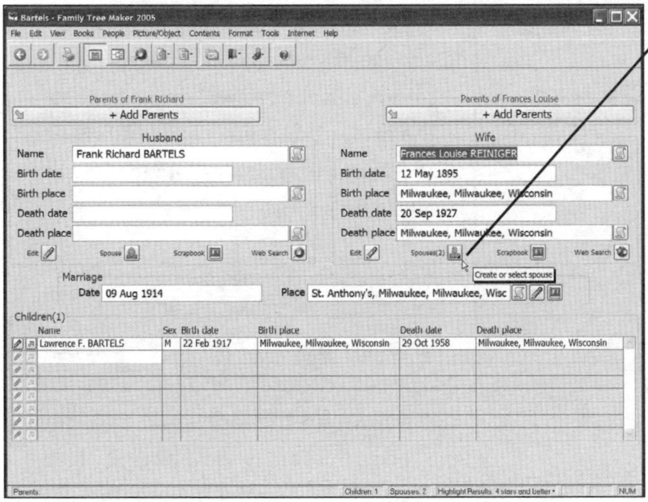

10. Click on the **Spouses** button. The Spouses dialog box will open.

11. Click the spouse for the marriage on which you want to work. The spouse will be highlighted.

12. Click **OK**. The Spouses dialog box will close and you will return to the Family View page with the alternate spouse you have selected. After viewing and making edits to the alternate spouse, if you leave this page, when you return, the spouse will revert back to the preferred spouse, and you will need to follow these steps again to view the alternate spouse.

> **TIP**
>
> Family Tree Maker will tell you how many children and spouses are known for the individual highlighted in the Family View page, by indicating the number in parentheses .

Creating a Relationship Between Parents and Children

You can indicate the child's relationship to each parent. You must first move the chosen individual into the child position in Family View, and then click in the field to select the name. This will not work if the individual is in the Husband or Wife position of Family View.

13. Click in the field that states the child's name.

14. Click on **People** from the **menu**. The People menu will open.

15. Click on **Other Parents** from the People menu. The Parents of dialog box will open. The top field lists all sets of parents associated with a child.

16. Click on a set of **parents**.

17. Click the drop-down arrow next to the **Relationship with father** field and click a relationship from the drop-down menu (natural, adopted, foster, etc.). The field will change to reflect the type of relationship you have chosen.

18. Click the drop-down arrow next to the **Relationship with mother** field and click a relationship. The field will change to reflect the type of relationship you have chosen.

19. Press **OK** when you have completed your selection, or click another set of parents to make additional changes. Or, press **Cancel** if you do not want to save your changes.

Viewing Other Family Groups

After you have entered information about a primary couple and their children, you may want to focus on a different family group. There are two main ways to navigate to a different family group:

Method 1: Use the navigation buttons in Family View.

Click on the **Parents** button, which is marked with a **blue arrow** or click on a blue arrow next to the child whose Family View you want to see. If there are more than eight children in your list, you may need to drag the **scroll bar** down until you find the desired child in the list.

The person selected will replace the person in the Husband or Wife field, and all of the other fields on the Family View page will change in accordance with the information currently known about that child.

Method 2: Use the Index of Individuals button.

Click on the **Index of Individuals** button in the toolbar to open the Index of Individuals dialog box.

1. Use the scroll bar on the right to scroll to the name, or enter the last name, comma, space, first name to search for a name in the Index of Individuals.

2. Make sure the name is highlighted; click on the **name** if it is not highlighted.

3. Click **Go to Family Page.** You will be taken to that individual's Family View, where that individual will be listed as the Husband or Wife.

TIP

You can also open the Index of Individuals dialog box by pressing the F2 key.

Adding More Details about an Individual

The Edit Individual dialog box was designed by combining the More About windows and the Individual Facts Card from previous versions of Family Tree Maker. The Edit Individual dialog box allows you to view and edit all the details you have entered into Family Tree Maker about an individual and to add details that do not fit elsewhere, e.g., religion, education, hobbies. You can access this feature through the Edit buttons, the People menu, or through certain charts and reports.

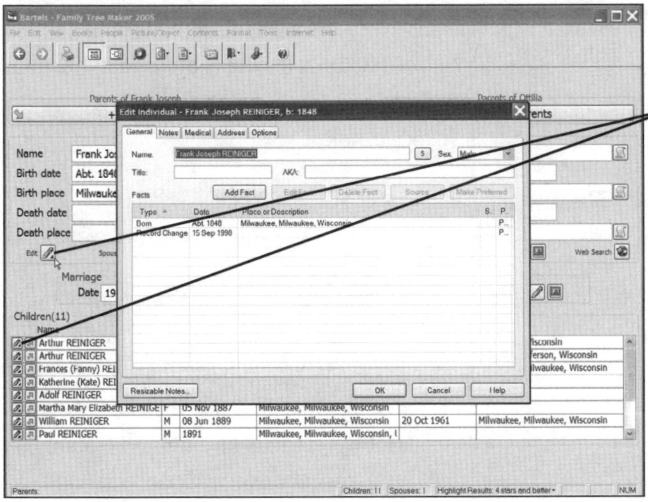

To open the Edit Individual dialog box from Family View:

1. Click on the **Edit** button near the Husband, Wife, or child. The Edit Individual dialog box for that individual will appear.

> ### TIP
>
> If you want to see the Edit Individual dialog box for a different individual, go to their Family View page first, by using the Index of Individuals button, then follow the above instructions. For example, for parents, click on their name to go to Family View, then select the **Edit** button from the Husband or Wife box.

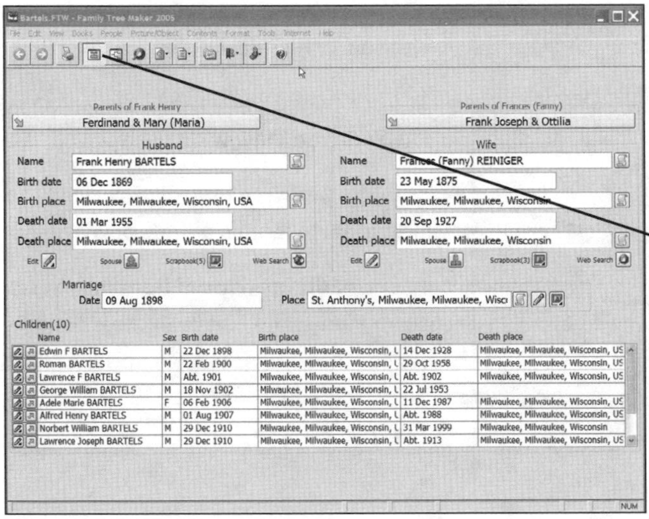

To open the Edit Individual dialog box from Pedigree View (you will learn more about Pedigree View in Chapter 4) there are two recommended options.

Method 1: Double-click.

1. Click on the **Pedigree View** button. The Pedigree View will appear.

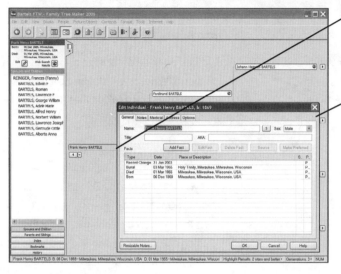

2. From the tree (not the Side Panel), double-click on the individual whose Edit Individual dialog box you would like to see.

3. The Edit Individual dialog box for that individual will appear.

NOTE

Later on, you will learn about using Preferences to change your default settings. One of the default options you can choose is that if you double-click on a name, you will be taken to the individual's Family View instead of the person's Edit Individual dialog box.

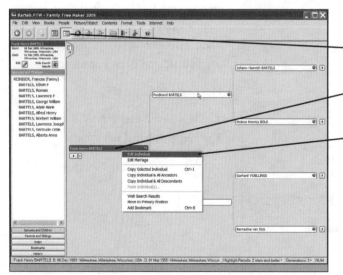

Method 2: Right-click.

1. Click on the **Pedigree View** button. The Pedigree View will appear.

2. In the pedigree tree, right-click on the individual to launch a drop-down menu.

3. Click **Edit individual** from the drop-down menu. The Edit Individual dialog box for that individual will appear.

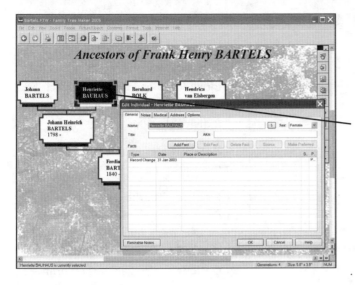

To open the Edit Individual dialog box from a Tree chart or report (The Edit Individual dialog box can be opened from any of the tree charts and most of the textual reports):

1. Double-click on the name of the person whose Edit Individual dialog box you would like to see.

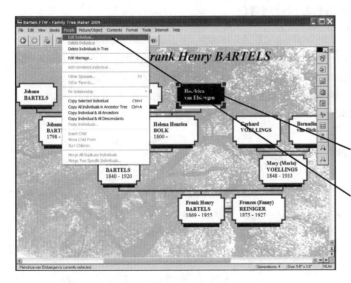

To open the Edit Individual dialog box from the People menu:

You can use the People menu to open an Edit Individual dialog box from anywhere in the program where an individual's name can be selected.

1. Click on the name to select the individual.

2. Go the **People** menu and click **Edit Individual**.

The Edit Individual dialog box contains five tabs:

- **General** – Name, sex, and title of the individual along with a list of facts and events. Enter general facts about the individual on this tab.

- **Notes** – Notes you want to add about the individual.

- **Medical** – Height, weight, cause of death and other medical information.

- **Address** – Address information.

- **Options** – Miscellaneous reporting and reference options.

Overview of the General Tab

When you first open an Edit Individual dialog box, the box will default to the General tab. The General section contains all of the basic information about an individual including name, sex, birth information, death information, and other facts. From this tab, you can add and edit all facts and sources associated with an individual, except relationships between individuals, which are noted in the Edit Marriage dialog box.

Resizing Columns

Although the columns in the General Tab are automatically sized, you can override this setting.

1. Place your cursor over the **Type/Date/Place** or **Description/S/P** bar. Move your cursor until it changes from a single arrow to one that points both right and left at the same time.

2. Hold down the left mouse button and drag the column right or left to increase or decrease the width of the column.

When you attempt to close the dialog box, Family Tree Maker will ask you if you want to override the automatic column sizing with column adjustments you have just made.

3. Click **Yes** if you want to override Family Tree Maker's automatic settings.

Change the Name or Add a Source

1. Click in the **AKA field** and type the name to add or edit a name, title, or nickname in the General Tab.

2. Click on the **source** button to add a source to the name. The Source-Citation dialog box will appear. See Chapter 6 for more details about adding sources.

Adding a Fact

1. Click **Add Fact**. The Add Fact dialog box will appear.

2. Click on the **drop-down arrow** next to Type. A list of events will appear. For practice, select **Occupation**. Press **tab** to go to the next line.

3. Enter a date in the **Date** field if you have a date you associate with the Fact Type. In this example, it may be the hire date. Press **tab** or click to go to the next line.

4. Type the description in the box labeled **Place or Description**. In this example, you might type "Farmer," or "accountant."

5. Press **OK** to save your fact and close the dialog box. Your new fact should appear in the list in the General section.

TIP

You can add a source citation to this fact. Highlight the fact and click on the Source button. See Chapter 6 for more details about adding source citations.

TIP

If you want to add a fact to the General tab that is not listed in the drop-down list, place your cursor in the Type field and type in your own fact name, e.g. Favorite Ice Cream, Awards Won, etc. Family Tree Maker will attempt to guess if you are trying to type in an existing fact, but ignore the suggestions and continue typing. Click tab when you are done to go to the next line and fill in the rest of the information about the fact.

Adding an Alternate Fact

You may have conflicting information about the same event, e.g., two different birth dates, but you can record both facts. This is especially valuable if you are unsure which fact is correct. If you have multiple facts for the same event, you must click a "preferred fact," which is the fact that will be displayed in the various views, charts, and reports. Typically, this is the fact that you believe to be most accurate. Other facts for the same event are referred to as "alternate facts" in Family Tree Maker. You can add alternate facts and change their status to preferred fact at any time. Create the alternate fact by adding it with the Add Fact button of the Edit Individual dialog box General Tab, just as you would when regularly Adding a Fact.

TIP

Alternate facts is one of the main reasons recording source information is so valuable.

To make the fact preferred:

1. Click on the alternate fact in the General Tab.

2. Click the Make Preferred button. The **Make Preferred** button is gray once you click it and the fact becomes preferred. The **P** in the right column of the fact also indicates its status as Preferred.

TIP

You can use the Date calculator to assist you in determining an exact date or age if you know two of three things: the age of the person at the time of death, marriage, or other event; the birth date; or the date of some other event. See Chapter 17 for more information.

NOTE

When entering a title in the General tab, do not enter such items as Jr. or III. The titles entered here will be printed in front of the individual's name on reports (e.g., III George Hunt instead of George Hunt III or Jr. George Hunt instead of George Hunt Jr.). If your ancestor was a Jr. or a Sr., this is typed into the Name field on the Family View page, at the end of the name and following a comma. When you are indexing your book, the comma becomes necessary in order to distinguish Jr. from the surname. Family Tree Maker automatically recognizes roman numerals such as III or IV, so no comma is necessary.

Entering Information in the Notes Tab

You may have family stories or other lengthy notes you want to preserve for future generations. Family Tree Maker's Edit Individual dialog box Notes tab addresses this need. This window allows you to enter details in a narrative style.

1. Click the **Notes** tab of the Edit Individual dialog box.

2. Enter the text you wish to include for the individual in the text box.

TIP

If you are typing information from another document on your computer into the Notes tab, you can usually "copy and paste" the text so you don't have to re-type existing text. For instance, if you are copying the text from a Word document into the Notes tab, highlight the text in the Word document, then press Ctrl+c to copy it. Then, go to the text box of the Notes tab and press Ctrl+v to paste your copy into that document.

TIP

The Notes field is limited in size, so it's best to save this area for anecdotal information, rather than source citations. With the sources feature, you can attach images of sources or use the text fields to record more detailed source information (see Chapter 6).

The Notes tab has three useful functions: Decrease, Increase, and Spell Check.

• **Decrease** – Click the **Decrease button** if you want to decrease the size of the text. This will allow you to fit more words on a page.

• **Increase** – Click the **Increase button** to increase the size of the text. This will make the text easier to read.

• **Spell Check** – Press the **Spell Check** button if you want to check your work. The Spell Check dialog box will open and start checking the this individual's notes for spelling errors.

– If Family Tree Maker detects a potential spelling error, it displays the error in the **Not in dictionary** field.

– Correct or ignore the word by using the Spell Check dialog box buttons. When a dialog box appears to tell you that the spell check is complete, click **OK**. You can tell Family Tree Maker to ignore capitalized words, words with numbers, and known names. To customize spell check's preferences, from the **File** menu, click **Preferences**, and then **Spell Check**.

NOTE

If you Close the Spell Check dialog box before the program has checked the entire Notes file, your spell check changes will not be saved.

> **NOTE**
>
> Family Tree Maker remembers the spell check you perform in a session, so if you attempt to spell check again, the spell checker will ignore the words you ignored in other spell checks of the file during the same session. When you close FTM and re-open the program, Family Tree Maker will check the words again. You will learn in Chapter 16 how to change your spell check preferences.

Printing Notes

Family Tree Maker notes print differently than other Family Tree Maker documents. Make sure you are in Family View and that you close the Edit Individual dialog box before attempting to print a note.

1. Open the **File** menu and click on **Batch Print Family View/Notes**. The Batch Print dialog box opens.

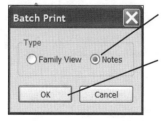

2. Click the **Notes** radio button from the Batch Print dialog box.

3. Press **OK**. The dialog box will close and the Individuals to Include in Batch Print dialog box will open.

4. Click on the name in the list on the left column of the Individuals to Include in Batch Print dialog box to select the individual whose note you want to print.

5. Press the **right angle bracket button** to move the individual to the right-hand column. You can select more than one individual by moving each individual from the left column to the right column.

6. Press **OK**.

7. The dialog box will close and the Batch Print More About Individual dialog box will open.

8. Press **OK**. The note will print. (Make sure you have your printer on).

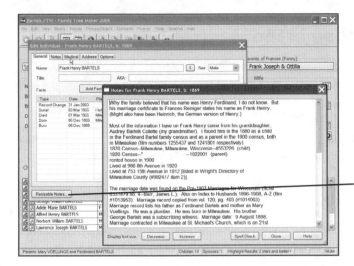

Resizable Notes

> **NOTE**
>
> The Resizable Notes button located at the bottom of the Edit Individual dialog box is available for each of the five tab views.

1. Click on the **Resizable Notes** button to open the **Notes for [name of individual]** dialog box. This contains all the details you have entered in the Notes tab.

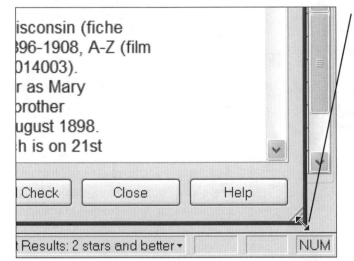

2. You may resize the **Notes for [name of individual]** dialog box to view all of your notes. Just place your mouse pointer on the lower right corner of the dialog box until the arrow turns into a double arrow, hold your left mouse button down, and drag the image right or left to increase or decrease the size of the box.

This dialog box also gives you the convenience of entering, comparing, and editing details in the Notes tab while viewing one of the other Edit Individual dialog box tabs. Just like in the regular Notes tab view, you can click the Increase and Decrease buttons to make the text larger and easier to read (Increase button) or smaller to fit more text (Decrease button). The Increase and Decrease buttons are for viewing convenience only and do not affect permanent settings or print jobs.

Entering Information in the Medical Tab

Knowing your family's health history can help you prevent and treat illnesses that run in family lines. The Medical tab helps you record basic medical details.

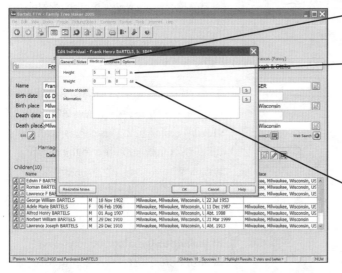

1. Click the **Medical** tab of the **Edit Individual dialog box**.

2. Click in the **height** field and type the height in feet and inches, by pressing the **tab** key to move from height to **feet**. Press the **tab** key again to move to the **weight** field. (You can also use your mouse to click in each field).

3. Enter the weight in **pounds** and **ounces** and press the **tab** key. The cursor will move to the **Cause of death** field.

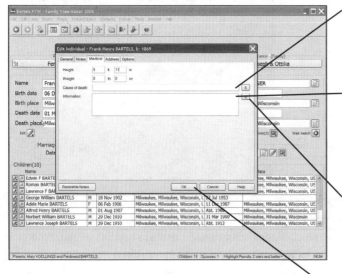

4. Enter a cause of death if it is known, or leave the field blank if not applicable. Press the **tab** key. The cursor will move to the **Medical information** field.

5. Enter any details you feel are important about the individual's medical history, from long-term illnesses to simple things, such as "suffers from hay fever," "prescribed glasses at age 15," etc.

6. Click the **S** button to go to the Source-Citation dialog box to record where you obtained any information you entered. Source-Citation dialog boxes will be covered more thoroughly in Chapter 6.

7. Click **OK** to close the Edit Individual dialog box.

Entering Information in the Address Tab

The Address tab is especially useful for recording the contact information of living relatives. However, it is also useful for researching records in an area where an ancestor was known to have lived.

1. Click on the **Address** tab of the Edit Individual dialog box. The Address window will be displayed.

2. Enter the street address in the **Street 1** field and press the tab key twice. The cursor will move to the City field.

3. Enter the city in the **City** field. Press the **tab** key. The cursor will move to the **State or province** field.

4. Enter the **State or province**. Press the **tab** key. The cursor will move to the **Zip or postal code** field.

5. Enter the **Zip or postal code**. Press the **tab** key. The cursor will move to the **Country** field.

6. Enter the country. Press the **tab** key. The cursor will move to the **Phone(s)** field.

7. Enter a phone number. Press the **tab** key. The cursor will move to the **E-mail(s)** field.

8. Type the e-mail address into the **E-mail(s)** field.

9. Press **OK** or **Cancel** to close the Edit Individual dialog box.

Using the Options Tab

The Options tab contains some miscellaneous settings, including a field for entering a reference number, the ability to exclude the individual from appearing on your calendars and the name format you wish to use for married women in reports and charts.

NOTE

You must also select the option to use married names in the specific report or chart; this only sets the format.

The reference number field allows you to enter any numbers or letters you choose. This reference system stems from the days when genealogy programs used numbers to find someone in the database. Today's software uses names, but some researchers still prefer to have the reference numbers available. This is useful if you use a unique filing or pedigree reference system. If you do not use such a system, leave the field blank. You may use a combination of letters and numbers up to 11 characters. You can also ask Family Tree Maker to automatically create a reference number for each individual in the Reference Numbers tab of the Preferences dialog box (see Chapter 17).

Adding Details about a Marriage in the Edit Marriage Dialog Box

You can add more details about a marriage through the Edit Marriage dialog box, including engagement and marriage details, and other marriage-related facts.

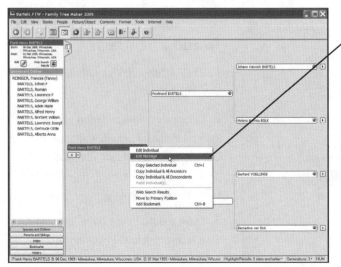

The dialog box is accessible from two main locations.

Method 1: Use the Family View

1. Click the **Edit** button located near the marriage information.

Or

Method 2: Use the Pedigree View

1. Click the right mouse button on an individual and select **Edit Marriage** from the drop-down menu.

The Edit Marriage dialog box contains two tabs: General and Notes. The General tab contains the basic information about the marriage (date, location). The Notes tab functions exactly the same as the Notes tab of the Edit Individual dialog box, including Resizable Notes, increasing and decreasing the text size, and spell check.

Entering Information in the Edit Marriage Dialog Box

The Edit Marriage dialog box has two relationship measures and a referencing system.

1. The **Kind of relationship** for the couple will default to **Married**. If this is not correct, click the Edit Marriage dialog box button, then click the **drop-down arrow** next to **Kind of Relationship** and **Status of Relationship** to choose from other options, e.g., friends, partners, unknown. Press **OK** to save changes.

2. The **Status of Relationship** box will default to **None**. If you want to change this status, click the drop-down arrow to choose from other options.

3. The **Reference number** field allows you to enter any numbers or letters you choose to keep track of marriages. This is the same function found under the Options tab of the Edit Individual dialog box, discussed earlier in this chapter.

To add a new fact:

1. Click **Add Fact**. The Add Fact dialog box will appear.

2. Click on the **drop-down arrow** next to Type. A list of events will appear. Choose the type of fact you would like to add, e.g., engagement, separation. Press the **tab** key.

3. Enter a date in the **Date** field, if a date is appropriate. Press the **tab** key.

4. Type descriptive information about the event (e.g,. location, type of degree, social security number) in the box labeled **Place or Description**.

5. Press **OK**. The information will be added to the list of facts on the Edit Individual dialog box and the Add Fact dialog box will close. To add a source citation to the fact, click on the fact, then click the **Source** button. See Chapter 6 for more details about adding source citations.

Edit a Fact in the Edit Marriage Dialog Box

1. Open the Edit Marriage dialog box, which should default to the General tab.

2. Click on the fact you would like edit.

3. Click the **Edit Fact** button.

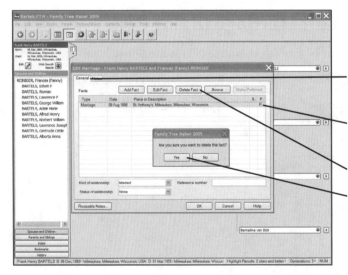

4. The Edit Fact dialog box will open.

5. Click on the drop-down arrow next to **Type** to change the type of fact, or, if the Type of fact is correct, press **tab** to go to the next line.

6. Highlight the date and type over it with the new date, or, if this is correct, press **tab** to go to the next line.

7. Change the information in the **Description** field if it is incorrect. Press **OK**.

Delete a Fact in the Edit Marriage Dialog Box

1. Open the Edit Marriage dialog box, which should default to the General tab.

2. Click on the fact you would like to delete.

3. Click the **Delete Fact** button.

4. Click **Yes** when Family Tree Maker asks, "Are you sure you want to delete this fact?" Your fact will be removed from the Facts list.

4

Editing Information about a Family

You may find errors in your entries or simply want to check for errors as you enter information, to make sure the details are as accurate as possible. Being accurate now will save yourself and those who may inherit your research headaches in the long run, and prevent incorrect facts from becoming accepted truths in your family history. In this chapter, you'll learn how to:

- Find individuals within the File
- Fix relationships
- Delete individuals from your Family File
- Check your Family File for data errors
- Merge duplicate individuals
- Use the spell checker
- Use Find and Replace

Editing Information in Family Tree Maker

As you continue to enter information about your family, you will want to use Family Tree Maker's editing features to check and correct your work.

Finding Individuals within the File

To quickly find a name in Family Tree Maker from the Family View:

1. Click **Find Individual** from the Edit menu. The Find Individual dialog box will open.

2. Choose which field in Family Tree Maker you want to search with the Search drop-down box. The Search box should default to Name; if not, make this selection from the drop-down menu.

3. Type the name of the individual in the **for** field, then press **Enter** or click **Find next**. The Family View page will switch to the individual you have selected.

> **TIP**
>
> You can also quickly find the individual you seek by using the Index of Individuals button in the toolbar covered in Chapter 3.

> **NOTE**
>
> If you are in the Pedigree View, you can use the Index section of the Side Panel or the Index of Individuals dialog box available through the toolbar.

Fixing Relationships

As you continue your research, you might discover you were mistaken on a marriage entry or on a parent-child relationship. This is especially likely to occur when you come across multiple generations of the same name (for instance, you may have confused John Smith with his grandson, also named John Smith).

Correcting a Marriage

1. Go to the **Family View** of the couple needing correction by using the **Find Individual** feature described above, or the **Index of Individuals**.

2. Click in the **Husband** or **Wife** field for the spouse you want to detach.

3. Click on the **People** menu and select **Fix Relationship**. A fly-out menu will appear.

4. Click on **Detach Spouse**. A dialog pop-up box will ask if you are sure you want to detach the spouse. If there are children associated with the couple, it also warns you that the children will no longer be associated with the individual being detached.

5. Click on **Yes** to confirm the change.

Linking Children to Parents

You might discover you have entered a child and his or her parents in the Family File, but you did not know they were related when you entered them. You can still link them together.

1. Click on an individual using the **Find Individual** feature described at the beginning of this chapter, or the Index of Individuals. This will take you to the **Family View** of the parent for whom you want to create a link.

2. Click on the **People** menu and select **Fix Relationship**. Another menu will appear.

3. Click on **Attach Child**. A dialog box containing an index of individuals will open.

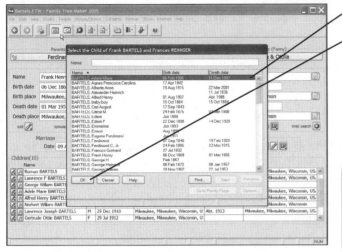

4. Click on the child from the list.

5. Click on **OK**. A message box will appear, verifying that you want to attach the individual as a child in Family View.

6. Click on **Yes** to associate the child with the parents.

NOTE

To sort children in Family View by age, click Sort Children from the People menu. Click OK. The children will be sorted from oldest to youngest.

Detaching a Child from the Wrong Parents

If you have incorrectly attached a child to parents, you can easily detach the child from the family. This will not delete the child from the Family File.

1. Go to the **Family View** of the family needing correction by using the **Find Individual** feature described at the beginning of this chapter or the **Index of Individuals**.

2. Click on the child you want to detach in the Children list.

3. Click on the **People** menu and select **Fix Relationship**. Another menu will appear.

4. Click **Detach Child**. If the child has siblings, a message will ask you if you want to detach them as well. After you click **Yes** or **No**, another message will confirm that you want to detach.

5. Click **Yes** to complete the operation. A final message will instruct you how to reattach the child if you change your mind.

Deleting Individuals From Your Family File

Detaching a spouse removes the individual from a marriage but not from the Family File. There are separate steps for deleting an individual, or deleting an entire group.

Caution

Deleting individuals from the Family File is permanent. You have one chance to bring the family members back after removing them, by using the **Undo** feature found under the **Edit** menu *immediately* after the deletion. You should create a backup of your Family File before deleting anyone by saving your file by another name. This way, if you do make a mistake, you will not lose valuable information.

Deleting a Single Individual

1. Select the person you want to delete from either Family View or Pedigree View.

2. Click on **Delete Individual** from the **People** menu. A dialog box will ask to confirm that you want to delete the individual.

3. Click **Yes** to delete the individual.

Deleting a Group of People

If you want to delete a group of individuals, you can do so using the tree charts. The group of individuals to be deleted must be visible on the chart in order for you to delete them as a group.

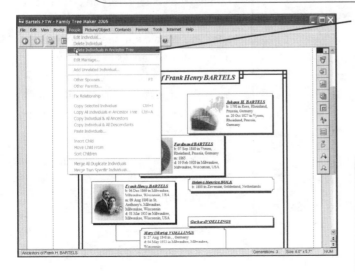

1. Click on the **Tree Charts** button in the toolbar. A drop-down menu listing various tree charts will appear.

2. Click on a chart style. The appropriate chart will appear.

TIP

You can also open a tree chart by clicking on the **View** menu, selecting **Tree Charts**, then clicking the chart from the fly-out menu.

NOTE

Look at the primary person on the report. It is important to verify if that primary person and those related to that person and displayed on the report are the individuals you wish to delete. If the person isn't the individual you want, you can use the Index of Individuals to select a new person (Use the toolbar button to open the Index of Individuals dialog box, and remain in the tree view you have selected. Select the correct individual in the list. Click **OK**.)

3. Click on the **People** menu and click **Delete Individuals** in <chart name>, where <chart name> is the type of chart you have open. A dialog box will appear, verifying you want to delete these individuals from your Family File.

NOTE

Remember that everyone who appears in the tree will be deleted. If you want to delete a single individual, you should not attempt to do it this way because you will lose other information.

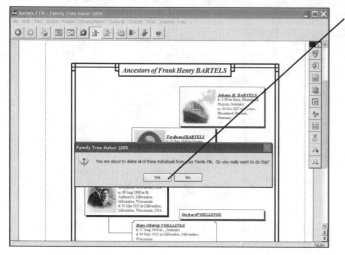

4. Click on **Yes** to delete all of the individuals in the chart from the Family File.

Checking the Family File for Data Errors

Family Tree Maker offers three different ways to check for errors: Data Entry Checking, Using the Find Error Command, and Working with the Data Errors Report.

Data Entry Checking

Family Tree Maker offers an error-checking feature that works automatically after you enable it in the preferences. It will check for errors as you enter information and alert you if it detects a possible error, such as an illegal character (e.g., *, &, #). To view or change your automatic error-checking settings:

1. Click on the **File** menu and click **Preferences**. The Preferences dialog box will open.

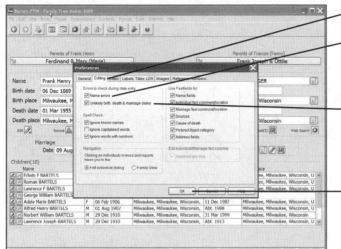

2. Click the **Editing** tab.

3. Click the **Name errors** check box to have Family Tree Maker check for name errors.

4. Click the **Unlikely birth, death, & marriage dates** check box to have Family Tree Maker check for date errors in those areas.

5. Click on **OK**. The error checking dialog box will close.

NOTE

When you type in a date that doesn't coincide with the other dates for an individual or family, Family Tree Maker will open a Data Entry Error message box to point out the problem, e.g., "death date is before birth date."

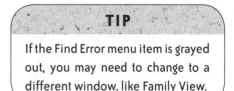

Using the Find Error Command

You can have Family Tree Maker search your entire file for errors and address them one at a time.

1. Click on the **Tools** menu and click **Find Error**. The Find Error dialog box will open.

TIP

If the Find Error menu item is grayed out, you may need to change to a different window, like Family View.

2. Click the errors for which you want to search. You can search for **Name errors** and/or **Unlikely birth, death, and marriage dates** by clicking the appropriate check box.

3. Click **OK**. Family Tree Maker will search your Family File for errors. When an error is found, you will have the following options:

NOTE

If you previously searched for errors and chose to ignore some of the potential problems found by Family Tree Maker, the **Reset all ignored errors** button will allow you to view them again.

a. Find Next – This will move you to the next error, saving any changes you may have made.

b. Close – Close the dialog box and stop checking for errors.

c. Help – Read Family Tree Maker help about this topic.

d. AutoFix – If the AutoFix button is not disabled, Family Tree Maker will fix the error based on what it thinks is most logical.

e. Ignore Error – Checking this box will make Family Tree Maker ignore that error indefinitely. You can always choose to view previously ignored errors again by opting to reset all ignored errors at the beginning of the Find Error process.

Find Error

The name may contain a nickname.

Name: Frances REINIGER

[Find next]
[Close]
[Help]
[Undo]
☐ Ignore error

TIP

If you click AutoFix in error, or if the change made by Family Tree Maker is not correct, click on **Undo**. The AutoFix button turns into the Undo button immediately after you make a fix, giving you an opportunity to change your mind. If you use the Undo feature, you will not move to the next error until you click on the **Find next** button. The Undo button only appears after you fix an error.

Working with the Data Errors Report

The Data Errors Report lists all potential errors that Family Tree Maker identifies in your Family File, including missing and illogical dates, individuals with no relations, duplicate individuals, and unrecognized characters or symbols.

1. Click the **Reports** toolbar button and click **Data Errors** from the drop-down menu.

TIP

You can also go to the **View** menu, click **Reports**, then **Data Errors**.

Bartels.FTW - Family Tree Maker 2005

File Edit View Books People Picture/Object Contents Format Tools Internet Help

Family Group Sheet
Outline Descendant
Genealogy Report
Kinship Report

Custom

Alternate Facts
Address
Medical Information
Birthdays of Living Individuals
Marriage
Parentage
Bibliography
Data Errors
Documented Events

Parents of Frank Henry   Parents of Frances (Fanny)
Ferdinand & Mary (Frank Joseph & Ottilia

Husband   Wife
Name   Frank Henry BARTELS   Name   Frances (Fanny) REINIGER
Birth date   06 Dec 1869   Birth date   25 May 1875
Birth place   Milwaukee, Milwaukee   Birth place   Milwaukee, Milwaukee, Wisconsin
Death date   01 Mar 1955   Death date   20 Sep 1927
Death place   Milwaukee, Milwaukee   Death place   Milwaukee, Milwaukee, Wisconsin

Marriage
Date 09 Aug 1898   Place St. Anthony's, Milwaukee, Milwaukee, Wis

Children(10)

Name	Sex	Birth date	Birth place	Death date	Death place
Edwin F BARTELS	M	22 Dec 1898	Milwaukee, Milwaukee, Wisconsin,	14 Dec 1928	Milwaukee, Milwaukee, Wisconsin, U
Roman BARTELS	M	22 Feb 1900	Milwaukee, Milwaukee, Wisconsin,	29 Oct 1958	Milwaukee, Milwaukee, Wisconsin, U
Lawrence F BARTELS	M	Abt. 1901	Milwaukee, Milwaukee, Wisconsin,	Abt. 1902	Milwaukee, Milwaukee, Wisconsin, U
George William BARTELS	M	18 Nov 1902	Milwaukee, Milwaukee, Wisconsin,	22 Jul 1953	
Adele Marie BARTELS	F	06 Feb 1906	Milwaukee, Milwaukee, Wisconsin,	11 Dec 1987	Milwaukee, Milwaukee, Wisconsin, U
Alfred Henry BARTELS	M	01 Aug 1907	Milwaukee, Milwaukee, Wisconsin,	Abt. 1988	Milwaukee, Milwaukee, Wisconsin, U
Norbert William BARTELS	M	29 Dec 1910	Milwaukee, Milwaukee, Wisconsin,	31 Mar 1999	Milwaukee, Milwaukee, Wisconsin, U
Lawrence Joseph BARTELS	M	29 Dec 1910	Milwaukee, Milwaukee, Wisconsin,	Abt. 1913	Milwaukee, Milwaukee, Wisconsin, U

Parents: Ottilia QUADE and Frank J REINIGER   Children: 10   Spouses: 1   Highlight Results: 2 stars and better ▾   NUM

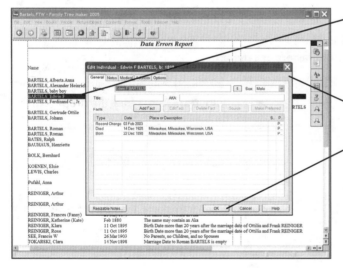

TIP

Notice the errors are listed in the third column of each row. You may want to select an individual (click once) in the list to more easily read the error.

2. Double-click on the individual to edit his or her information. The Edit Individual dialog box for the individual will appear.

3. Correct the error in the Edit Individual dialog box if known.

4. Click **OK** to close the Edit Individual dialog box and return to the next error in the Data Errors Report.

NOTE

The Data Errors report is also discussed in Chapter 9.

Moving Information to Another Location

Family Tree Maker allows you to use the standard Windows Copy and Paste functions to move text from field to field. For this to work, you must be in a field where text can be selected, for example, Family View.

1. Place the mouse in front of the first character you want to select, hold down the left mouse button, and drag the mouse until you reach the last character you wish to cut or copy. The selected text will be highlighted. In some windows, you cannot drag your mouse over a select amount of characters but clicking once will still allow you to select the text.

2. Click on the **Edit** menu and select **Copy Text**. (Or, select **Cut Text** to remove the text item from the field. The selected text will be removed from the field but you will still be able to copy it to a new location.)

3. Go the field where you want to place the information.

4. Click on the **Edit** menu and click **Paste Text**. The text you just copied or cut will be moved to the new field.

NOTE

To move a child to a different location in the Children list in Family View, click on the child you want to move, then click the People menu, then click Move Child From. Follow the instructions that will appear in the dialog box.

Merging Duplicate Individuals

Family Tree Maker offers a method to merge individuals that looks not only at the name of the individuals, but also at additional information, such as family relationships and dates of events. You must be in **Family View** for the Merge Duplicates options to be enabled on the **People** menu.

1. Click **People** to open the People menu.

2. Click **Merge All Duplicate Individuals**. A message box will appear, reminding you to back up your file before you merge duplicate individuals.

TIP

You should make it a practice to back up your Family File before you do anything major to the file. For more on saving back up files, see Chapter 15 "Working with Other Family Files."

3. Click **No** if you do not wish to back up at this time,. The Merge All Duplicate Individuals dialog box will open.

NOTE

If Family Tree Maker cannot find duplicates, a message box will appear, telling you that none were found.

4. Click on **View/Print Detailed Merge Report**. The Merge Individuals and Sources Report window (labeled Merge Individuals Report) will appear.

> **TIP**
>
> You can click on a line in the list to obtain additional information regarding differences between two possible duplicates.

5. Click **Close**. The Merge All Duplicate Individuals dialog box will reappear.

> **NOTE**
>
> If you have a particularly lengthy list of potential duplicates, it is a good idea to print out this report before going ahead with the additional steps. This way you have a printed record of the duplicates Family Tree Maker merged.

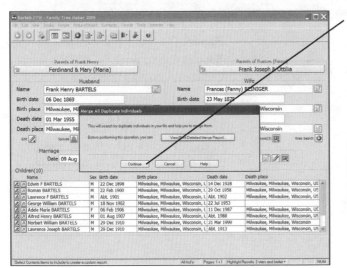

6. Click **Continue**. The Merge All Duplicate Individuals dialog box will close, and the Likely Matches dialog box will open with all matches selected for merging.

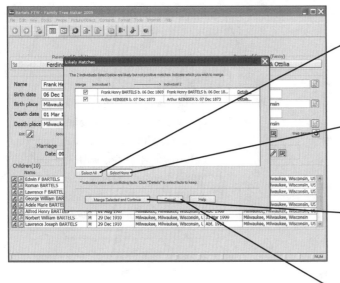

7. Choose from the following options:

a. Click **Select All**. The check box next to each pair of likely matches will be selected. Click **Details** for more information (see step 8 and 9).

b. Click **Select None**. The check box next to each pair of likely matches will be empty. Click **Details** for more information (see step 8 and 9).

c. Click **Merge Selected and Continue**. Family Tree Maker merges the likely pairs that have a check in their check box. Click Close when the operation is complete.

d. Click **Cancel**. A dialog box will verify you want to cancel. Click **Yes**. The Likely Matches dialog box will close and the merge will be canceled.

8. Click **Details**. The Merge Individuals dialog box will open.

Use the Merge Individuals dialog box to compare information between the two names before completing the Family Tree Maker merge.

9. Choose one of the following options:

a. Click **Merge**. The individuals will be merged and the Likely Matches dialog box will close.

b. Click **Merge and go to Next Pair**. The individuals will be merged and the details for the next pair of individuals in the Likely Matches dialog box will be shown.

c. Click **Skip to Next Pair**. The individuals will not be merged and the details for the next pair of individuals in the Likely Matches dialog box will be shown.

d. Click **Cancel**. The individuals will not be merged and the Merge Individuals dialog box will close.

Merging Two Specific Individuals

Instead of checking for duplicate individuals, you can also merge two specific individual records that you know are duplicates. To do this you must be in Family View.

1. Click on the name you know has duplicate information.

2. From the **People** menu, click **Merge Two Specific Individuals**. Then Select the individual who is the same as [the name you selected in step 1] dialog box will open.

3. Click the duplicate individual from the list, using the scroll bar to move up and down the list, or typing in the last name, comma, space, then first name.

Press **OK**. Family Tree Maker will open a dialog box verifying the information. Select **Yes**.

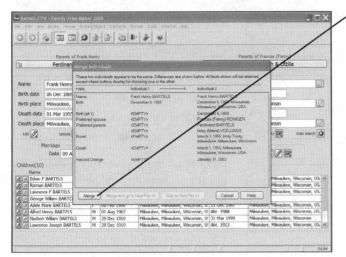

The **Merge Individuals dialog box** will open. Press **Merge** to complete the Merge.

TIP

After you have merged individuals, Family Tree Maker will remind you that you can undo the merge, provided that you do it before you make any further changes to the family file. Click on **View/Print Detailed Merge Report** and then print out and read through the Merge Report to make sure everything was merged correctly.

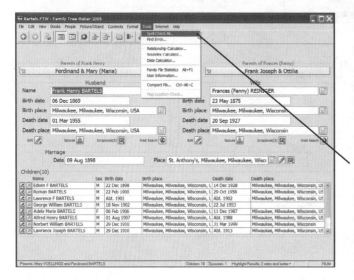

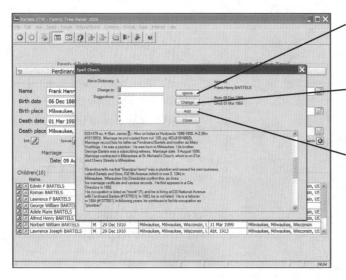

Using the Spell Checker

Use the spell checker feature to catch spelling errors in your Family File. Family Tree Maker spell checks your Books and your Edit dialog boxes separately.

1. Click on the **Tools** menu and click **Spell Check All**. The Spell Check dialog box will open and Family Tree Maker will move to the first screen and highlight the first word not found in the Family Tree Maker dictionary. The following options are available:

a. Ignore – This will ignore the word and move to the next word Spell Check finds.

b. Change –This will replace the highlighted word with the word listed in the Change field.

c. Add – This will place the highlighted word in the dictionary so Family Tree Maker recognizes the word as an acceptable word and does not consider it misspelled. You may want to do this with certain names that appear frequently in your notes since the spell checker will not recognize surnames and city names.

TIP

If the dictionary does not supply you with the appropriate choice, you can type the word in the **Change to** field and then click on the **Change** button. Family Tree Maker will make the change.

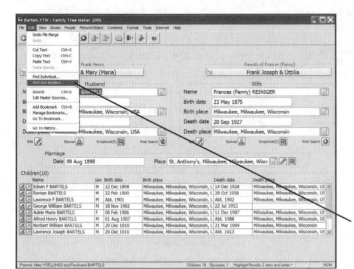

Using Find and Replace

You may have inadvertently spelled a city or other word wrong throughout the Family File. You can use Family Tree Maker's Find and Replace feature to correct this mistake quickly and easily over the entire Family File, rather than looking for each occurrence of the same error.

1. Click **Find and Replace** in the **Edit** menu. The Find and Replace dialog box will open.

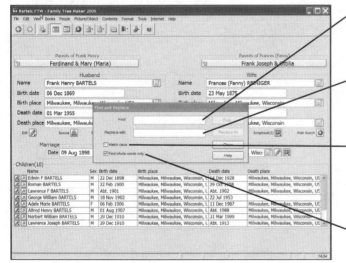

2. Type the word or name that you want to change in the **Find** field. Press **tab** to move to the next field.

3. Type the word or name you would like to use in place of the word in the Find field, in the **Replace with** field.

4. Click the **Match case** box if you only want Family Tree Maker to find words that match exactly (upper and lower case letters).

5. Click the **Find whole words only** box if you only want Family Tree Maker to find matching words (for example, if you asked for "Will," Family Tree Maker would not show results for "William").

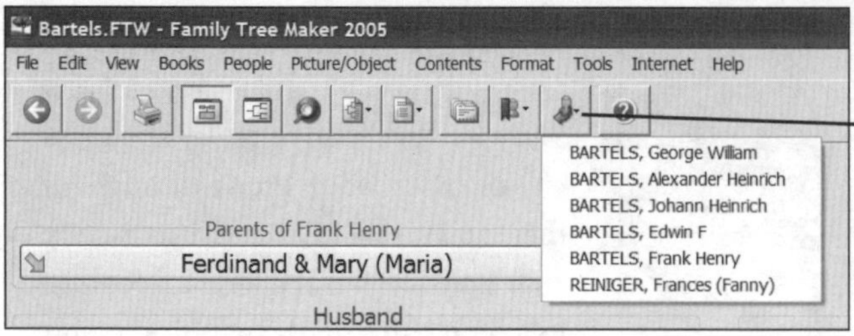

Bartels.FTW - Family Tree Maker 2005

File   Edit   View   Books   People   Picture/Object   Contents   Format   Tools   Internet   Help

BARTELS, George Willam
BARTELS, Alexander Heinrich
BARTELS, Johann Heinrich
BARTELS, Edwin F
BARTELS, Frank Henry
REINIGER, Frances (Fanny)

Parents of Frank Henry

Ferdinand & Mary (Maria)

Husband

NOTE

You can view your most recently edited individuals by viewing your editing history. Click the **History** button from the toolbar for a drop-down menu of recently edited individuals, or go to the **Edit** menu and click **Go To History** for a history dialog box of the last 30 individuals you have edited. In either case, the individual you select will become the primary individual in whatever window you have open (e.g., if you Go To History from Family View, you will go to that individual's Family View page).

5

Navigating and Editing in Pedigree View

Pedigree View, the second main view in Family Tree Maker, complements Family View by allowing you to view, browse, and edit up to seven generations of your family tree at a time so you can take a comprehensive look at your progress on your family tree, quickly establish relationships between individuals, and organize your research with the various functions of the program. In this chapter, you'll learn how to:

- Change the primary individual in Pedigree View
- Navigate the Pedigree View tree
- Use the Pedigree View Side Panel
- Edit in Pedigree View

Pedigree View is new to Family Tree Maker 2005. While Family View focuses on a single-family unit, Pedigree View offers a more comprehensive view of your family tree, allowing you to view from three to seven generations at once. You can navigate within the tree, view details about individuals, check for Web Search results regarding each individual, edit and add details, and more. The Side Panel provides additional navigation and details about an individual and his/her immediate family. This chapter will cover the various features in Pedigree View.

> **NOTE**
>
> Family Tree Maker has a standard pedigree chart that is not navigable, which should not be confused with the Pedigree View.

Opening Pedigree View

Click the **Pedigree View** button on the toolbar to open Pedigree View.

> **TIP**
>
> You can also go to Pedigree View by going to the **View** menu and clicking **Pedigree View**.

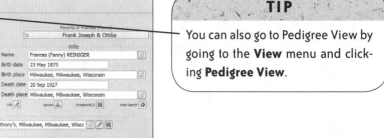

Navigating the Tree in Pedigree View

Changing the primary or root individual

Since Pedigree View only shows the direct ancestors of the primary individual, you may want to switch the primary individual to view a different ancestor line, or you may want to switch primary individuals to view ancestors further up the ancestral line.

Even though a family member in your Family File is not in the current line in your Pedigree View, you can still view family members in the Side Panel, as will be covered later in this chapter.

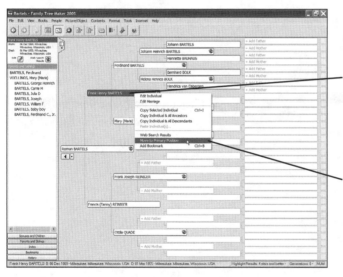

To move an individual in the current tree display to the position of primary individual:

1. Right-click on the node listing the individual you want to be the primary individual from the tree. A menu will appear either above or beneath the node.

2. Click **Move to Primary Position**. Animation will indicate how the individuals are shifting within the tree as the individual is moved to the Primary position.

NOTE

If you navigate through one generation at a time, animation will help prevent you from getting lost by showing you how the people move within the tree. Animation is slower the first few times you navigate within your Pedigree View tree so you can easily see and understand how it works. After the first few times, animation speeds up.

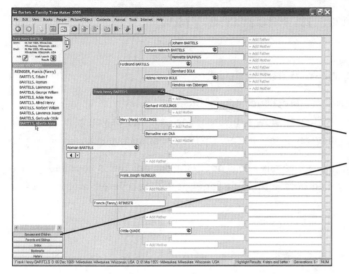

If the individual you want to see become the primary individual is not in the current tree but is an immediate family member (i.e., a spouse, sibling, or child of an individual in the current view):

1. Click on the individual in the chart.

2. Click **Spouses and Children** or **Parents and Siblings** from the Side Panel, depending on what is appropriate. The button will expand in the Side Panel.

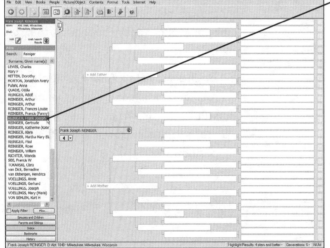

3. Click once on the desired individual. The individual will become the primary individual in the tree.

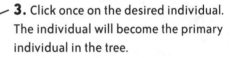

You can also go to any individual in your Family File by using the Index option in the Side Panel.

1. Click on the **Index** button in the Side Panel. This will bring up a list of all the individuals you have entered into Family Tree Maker.

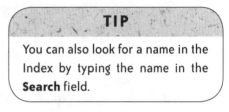

2. Scroll to find the appropriate individual.

> ## TIP
>
> You can also look for a name in the Index by typing the name in the **Search** field.

3. Click once on the desired individual. The individual will become the primary individual in the tree.

Changing the Number of Generations in Pedigree View

You can view three to seven generations in Pedigree View at a time. The more generations you add, the smaller the names will appear in the chart, but the more ancestors you will be able to view at once.

> ## NOTE
>
> If you choose the seven-generation option, the names will be too small to be legible. However, you can use your mouse to "hover" over the node without clicking to view bubble help, which will provide the name, birth, and death information for the individual if you have entered this information in your Family File. The six and seven generation views are useful for quickly determining where more research is needed, or where there are holes in your family tree.

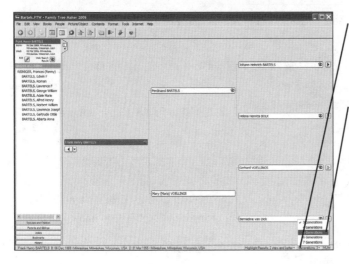

1. Click on the drop-down arrow labeled **Generations** in the status bar at the bottom right section of the screen. A menu will appear.

2. Click the number of generations you would like the chart to display. The Pedigree View chart will change to reflect the number of generations you chose.

Web Search Results in Pedigree View

A small Web Search icon will appear next to each name in the chart node if an individual meets a search criteria that you set, with one star being a possible match and five stars being an extremely likely match. You can change your Web Search criteria at any time. (Learn more about Web Search in Chapter 11).

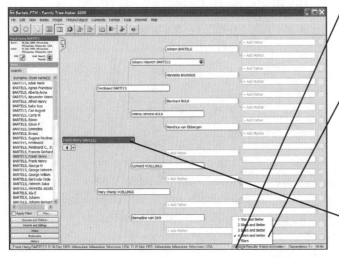

1. Click on the drop-down arrow labeled **Highlight Results** in the status bar at the bottom right section of the screen. A menu will appear.

2. Click the number of stars you would like (i.e., the quality level of the match) before Family Tree Maker displays the Web Search icon on an individual's node. A check mark will appear next to the item you chose.

3. The Pedigree View will show Web Search result icons wherever search results for an individual have met these conditions.

Understanding Navigation Arrows

• **Solid navigational arrows** – indicate that more ancestors are available to view in the pedigree tree that do not fit in the allotted number of generations displaying in the current chart. Arrows pointing to older generations are located to the right of the pedigree.

The arrow pointing to the left under the primary individual will shift the tree to the descendants of that person. By default, Family Tree Maker will move down through your tree via the same path you traversed up your tree. If you haven't previously navigated to the descendants of the primary person, Family Tree Maker will automatically go to the child with descendants. If more than one child has descendants, Family Tree Maker will then look at the previous generation. If Family Tree Maker still can't determine the most probable path, the program will display a drop-down list of children for you to choose. At any time, you can click on the drop-down arrow below the primary individual to choose a child of the primary person rather than waiting to see which path Family Tree Maker will choose by default.

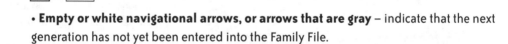

• **Empty or white navigational arrows, or arrows that are gray** – indicate that the next generation has not yet been entered into the Family File.

• **Down arrow** –lists all the descendants of the root individual. Click on a name from the list to make the child the new primary individual.

> **NOTE**
>
> The drop-down list of descendants will only display the children of the individual's preferred marriage if the individual has more than one spouse in the Family File.

> **TIP**
>
> You can use keyboard buttons to navigate the tree.
>
> • In the pedigree tree, use the right and left arrow to move from one column to the next.
>
> • Use the up and down arrow to move up and down a column.
>
> • Use the tab key to move from the pedigree tree to the buttons and tabs in the Side Panel.

Using the Pedigree Side Panel

The Side Panel offers both navigational shortcuts as well as useful contextual information about the individuals in the tree.

Opening and Closing the Side Panel

The Side Panel is expandable and contractible.

1. Click the tab to the top right of the Side Panel to open or close the panel.

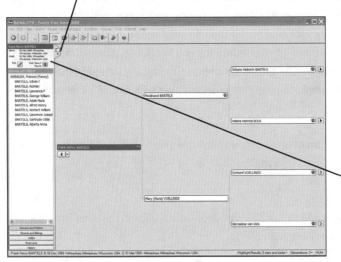

Exploring the Side Panel

The Side Panel contains six major sections specific to the selected individual (which does not need to be the primary/root individual. Just click once on a name in the tree to select the individual):

1. Details – Located at the top of the Side Panel, Details will display the basic information about the selected individual, such as birth and death information. In addition, you can click the Edit button to open the Edit Individual dialog box or the Web Search Results button to visit the Web Search page. This section remains visible as long as the Side Panel is expanded.

NOTE

If the birth and death fields are blank, but the christening and/or burial dates have been entered (see Chapter 3), these dates will appear in the details section in place of the birth and death dates. Since initiations into a religion can occur later in life, Family Tree Maker uses the "christening" fact to represent a beginning of life date, while the baptism fact can be used if it occurred later in life.

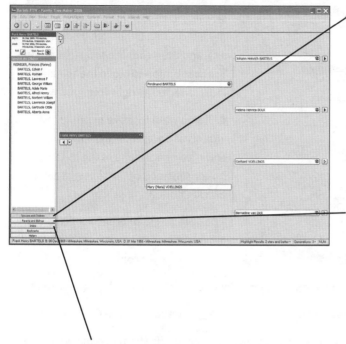

2. Spouses and Children – This section contains a list of the spouse(s) and children of the selected individual for both reference as well as easier navigation. To view basic information about any of these individuals, select one of the names (scroll over without clicking) in the list and a pop-up will appear listing details. If you click on the name, the name will be moved to the root position in the tree.

3. Parents and Siblings – This section contains the list of parents and siblings of the selected individual. To view basic information about any of these individuals, scroll over one of the names with your mouse. If you click on the name, the name will be moved to the root position in the tree.

4. Index – This section contains a list of all of the individuals in your file. Just click on a name to jump to the pedigree tree of anyone in the list. You can use the scrollbar to move down the list, or you can type a name in the search box (last name, space, first name) to jump to a particular person. You can also filter this list to show a subset of individuals, which can be useful if your file is very large and you want to focus on a particular line.

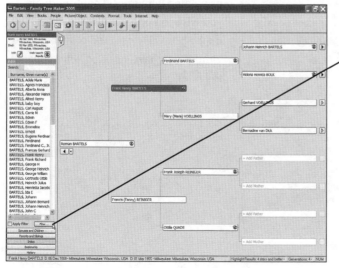

To create and apply a filter in the Side Panel Index:

a. Click on the **Filter** button in the Side Panel (only visible when in Index mode). The Individuals to Include dialog box will appear.

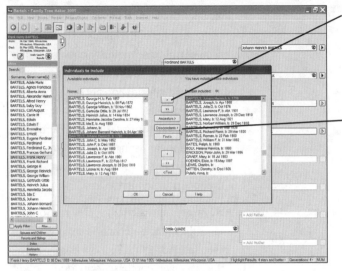

b. Click to choose the individual from the left column (Available individuals), and then click the **top right angle bracket** button to move the selected individual to the right column.

c. If you want to move multiple individuals at once, click an individual and then choose one of the following buttons instead of the top right angle bracket button:

• **Double angle bracket >>** button to move every individual from the left column to the right column.

• **Ancestors>** button to move all of the chosen individual's ancestors to the right column

• **Descendants>** button to move all of the individual's descendants to the right column

• **Find>** button to specify a category type in which all individuals should be moved to the right column, e.g., all individuals born in a certain location, or who are all the same gender. (The Add Individuals dialog box will open. Click a category type from the Search drop-down menu, then click **OK**.)

d. Click **OK** when the right column is populated with the set of individuals you wish to appear in the index list. The dialog box will close, and only the individuals you have selected will appear in the filter.

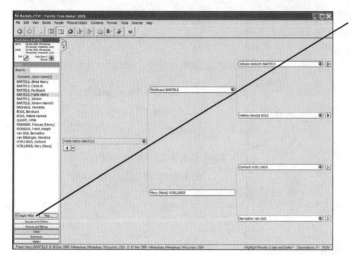

e. You can always turn the filter off by removing the check mark from the **Apply Filter** box (click inside the box) if you wish to see the entire list again.

6. Bookmarks – This section contains a list of all individuals you have specifically book-marked as individuals you want to be able to find quickly in your Family File. Just click on a name to jump to the Pedigree View of anyone in the list.

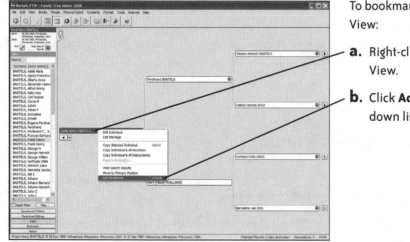

To bookmark an individual in Pedigree View:

a. Right-click on a name in Pedigree View.

b. Click **Add Bookmark** from the drop-down list.

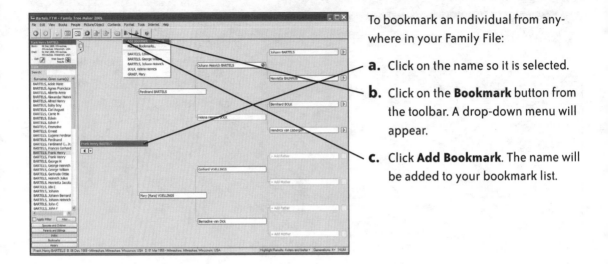

To bookmark an individual from any-where in your Family File:

a. Click on the name so it is selected.

b. Click on the **Bookmark** button from the toolbar. A drop-down menu will appear.

c. Click **Add Bookmark**. The name will be added to your bookmark list.

7. History – This section lists the individuals you have viewed most recently in your Family File. If you click on a name in the list, the name will be moved to the root position in the tree.

NOTE

An individual will automatically be added to your History list if you open his or her Edit Individual dialog box and click **OK**. If you do not make changes, click **Cancel** to avoid having the individual added to your History list.

Editing in Pedigree View

Add New Individuals to Pedigree View

If an empty node (no information entered about the individual) follows directly after a completed node (information has been entered about the individual) in Pedigree View, the node will be labeled **+Add Father** or **+Add Mother**. There are two recommended ways to add this information.

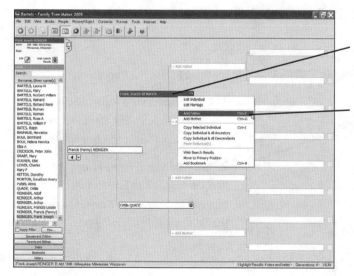

Method 1: Click an empty node.

1. Click the **+Add Father** or **+ Add Mother** node. The Add Mother of dialog box or the Add Father of dialog box will open. These dialog boxes function the same as the Edit Individual dialog box discussed in Chapter 3.

2. Enter the Father or Mother's name in the **Name** field, in the same order you would enter the information in the Name field of Family View.

3. Click **OK** when you are done. The dialog box will close and the information will be added.

Or

Method 2: Right-click an individual.

1. Right-click on the individual for whom you would like to add a father or a mother.

2. Click **Add Father** or **Add Mother** from the drop-down menu. Fill in the Edit Individual dialog box with details about the new individual the same way as in step 3a.

Add or Edit Details about Individuals in Pedigree View

Add or edit details about an individual by opening the Edit Individual dialog box you learned about in Chapter 3. There are a few ways to open the Edit Individual dialog box from Pedigree View, including the method you just learned to open the Father and Mother's Edit Individual dialog box.

Method 1: Double-click the individual

1. Double-click the individual you would like to edit. The individual's Edit Individual dialog box will appear. Click **Cancel** to close the Edit Individual dialog box.

Or

Method 2: Use the People menu.

1. Click once on the individual you would like to edit. The field will be highlighted, indicating it has been selected.

2. Click **Edit Individual** from the **People** menu. The Edit Individual dialog box will appear. Click **Cancel** to close the Edit Individual dialog box.

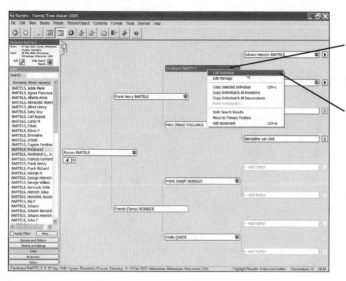

Or

Method 3: Right-click.

1. Right-click once on the individual you would like to edit. A drop-down menu will appear.

2. Click **Edit Individual**. The individual's Edit Individual dialog box will appear. Click **Cancel** to close the Edit Individual dialog box.

6

Documenting Sources

Citing the sources of your family history information is one of the most important aspects of your research. Citing sources helps you keep track of the records you have used, which helps you avoid wasting time revisiting sources. In this chapter, you'll learn how to:

- Create a Master Source
- Create a Source Citation
- Attach an image to a source
- View, display, and print source information

With Family Tree Maker, you can cite sources for the names of individuals and specific events. You can also cite multiple sources for each fact. This allows you to compare conflicting information, keep track of which sources you have researched, and compare notes with other researchers. When possible, you should cite a source for every name and fact you enter.

Understanding Master Sources and Source Citations

Family Tree Maker allows you to create both "Master" sources and source citations, to prevent you from typing in the same source information multiple times. For example, you may want to cite a particular book as a source for several different pieces of information. The basic information about the book (title, author, publication information) is the same for every citation, but you may have found information in several places throughout the book.

- The master source dialog box stores unchanging facts such as the author, title, and publication information for a book, so you can quickly recall them when entering information in the source-citation dialog box, rather than typing the same fact over and over.

- The source-citation dialog box allows you to record individual source citation details for each fact and individual you enter.

Creating a Master Source

1. Click on the **Edit** menu and select **Edit Master Sources**. The Master Source dialog box will open.

> **NOTE**
>
> You can also create a Master Source from the Source-Citation dialog box, which will be covered later in this chapter. After you enter information in the Source-Citation dialog box **Title of source** field, the **Edit Master Source** button will be activated. You can click on the **Edit Master Source** button to open the Master Source dialog box.

2. Type the title of the source in the **Title of source** field and press the **Tab** key. The rest of the fields will be activated and the cursor will move to the Author/Originator field.

After you enter your first Master Source, the next time you open the Master Source dialog box, it will pre-populate with that information. You can use the **next** and **previous** arrows to see what other master source information you have entered, or you can click **New** to start a new master source.

NOTE

In most cases, the title of the source will print out in italics when source citations are included on reports.

3. Type the author's name in the **Author/Originator** field and press the **Tab** key. The cursor will move to the **Publications facts** field.

4. Type the publication information.

NOTE

Publication information includes the place of publication, the name of the publishing company, and the copyright date, e.g., Provo, Utah: MyFamily.com, Inc., 2005.

5. Click the type of media from the **Source media** drop-down menu.

NOTE

Including the source media type will help you later if you want to view the source again.

6. Type the call number in the **Call number** field if one exists, and press the **Tab** key. The cursor will move to the **Source location** field.

NOTE

The call number is the number assigned to the source in the repository where it was found. This could be a microfilm number, a Dewey Decimal system number, or some other numbering system unique to that particular library or archive.

7. Type the source location and press the **Tab** key. The cursor will move to the **Comments** field.

NOTE

The source location is wherever the original source exists, so you can return to it if you need to revisit the original. This could be a library, archive, county courthouse, or cousin's residence, for example.

8. Type your comments and press the **Tab** key. The cursor will move to the **Source quality** field.

NOTE

Use the Comments section to record any additional thoughts about the source and information. This information will not print on your reports; it is for your personal reference.

9. Type the quality of the source.

NOTE

The quality of the source is one reference to the reliability of the source. You can use this field to note both the legibility of the source as well as its potential accuracy (i.e., primary source, secondary source, family legend, etc.).

10. Click on **OK**. The Master Source dialog box will close.

Creating a Source Citation

The Source-Citation dialog box is where you will select the appropriate master source for the information you are citing. You can enter source information when you enter the data and details for each ancestor in Family View.

1. Click on the **Source/Citation** button next to the field for which you want to add a source citation, for example, the source citation for an individual's name. The Source-Citation dialog box will open.

NOTE

You can also open the Source-Citation dialog box from the Edit Individual dialog box or Edit Marriage dialog box, by highlighting the appropriate fact and clicking on the **Source** button.

2. Or, click **Source** from the **Edit** menu, or press **Ctrl+S**. The Source-Citation dialog box will open. The source citation will be attached to the highlighted field or the last field in which you were working.

3. Click on the **Find Master Source** button. The Find Master Source dialog box will open.

4. Click on the name of the Master source to select the master source from the Find Master Source dialog box.

TIP

If you have a lengthy list of sources, you can type part of the title in the Title field, and Family Tree Maker will highlight the first title that matches.

5. Click **OK**. The Find Master Source dialog box will close.

NOTE

Notice that the title of the source and the printed format of the footnote are now displayed in the Source-Citation dialog box.

Source-Citation (1 of 1): Name for Ferdinand BARTELS   ✕

New	Delete

First   Prev.   Next   Final

Master Source Information

Title of source: 1930 United States Federal Census

Find Master Source...   Edit Master Source...

Citation Information

Citation Page: Add Image...   View Image...

Citation Text:

☑ Include citation text in footnote   Restore footnote

Footnote: (Printed format)   1930 United States Federal Census, Provo, UT: Ancestry.com, 2001.

OK   Cancel   Help

---

6. Type the page number of the citation in the Citation Page field if applicable.

NOTE

Not all source citations will have a page number included on this screen. Elizabeth Shown Mills's *Evidence! Citation and Analysis for the Family Historian* (Genealogical Publishing Co., 1997) is a well-accepted reference for sourcing your genealogical research.

7. Type the Citation text in the **Citation Text** field if desired. The citation text might be additional identifying information. For instance, when citing a census record, you would want to include the Enumeration District, Supervisor's District, Dwelling number, and Family number for the specific house of your ancestor on that census page.

Source-Citation (1 of 1): Name for Ferdinand BARTELS   ✕

New	Delete

First   Prev.   Next   Final

Master Source Information

Title of source: 1930 United States Federal Census

Find Master Source...   Edit Master Source...

Citation Information

Citation Page: Add Image...   View Image...

Citation Text:

☑ Include citation text in footnote   Restore footnote

Footnote: (Printed format)   1930 United States Federal Census, Provo, UT: Ancestry.com, 2001.

OK   Cancel   Help

TIP

You can decide whether to include text from the Citation Text field in the printed footnote. Click on the **Include citation text in footnote** check box if you want the text to be included. If the text is just for your information, make sure the box is not checked.

8. Click on **OK** to close the Source-Citation dialog box.

Creating Additional Source Citations

You can create more than one source citation for the same fact.

1. Open the Source-Citation dialog box for which you want to add an additional source citation.

2. Click **New**. The citation fields will become blank, but you will not lose the source information you already entered.

3. Enter the new source information and then press **OK**. The source-citation dialog box will close.

4. Open the source. The bar across the top will indicate how many sources have been entered for the fact. Click the **First**, **Prev**, **Next**, or **Final** arrow buttons to toggle between the sources.

Attaching an Image to a Source

Family Tree Maker allows you to attach images to your sources, in a manner similar to how you attach images to charts, reports, and the scrapbook. Scrapbooks are the main area in which you will work with images, as will be covered in a later chapter.

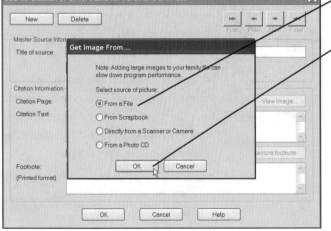

Husband	
Name	Ferdinand BARTELS
Birth date	07 Sep 1840
Birth place	Vynen, Rheinland, Prussia, Germany
Death date	19 Feb 1920
Death place	Milwaukee, Milwaukee, Wisconsin, USA

Edit   Spouse   Scrapbook(5)   Web Search

1. Click on the **Source** button next to the name in Family View. The Source-Citation dialog box will open.

2. Click on the **Add Image** button. The **Get Image from** dialog box will open.

3. Click the appropriate source of the picture. The option will be selected.

4. Click on **OK**. Family Tree Maker will open a window or launch the appropriate program.

5. Click the image from the window and press **Open**. The Edit Picture dialog box will open.

6. Click **OK**. The image will be added to your source.

7. Click the **View Image** button to view the image.

Viewing, Displaying, and Printing Source Information

You can view source information the same way you entered it, by visiting the Source-Citation dialog box. This dialog box appears when you click the **Source** button to the right of each name or fact in Family View, or when you select the item, then select **Source** from the **View** menu.

You can also display and print your source information in select reports:

Print source information from one of the reports listed below by clicking the **Print** button from the toolbar while the report is open, and selecting **OK** from the Print dialog box.

• The Bibliography report lists all sources you have entered in your Family File (see Chapter 8).

• The Documented Events report lists all events for which you have entered source information (see Chapter 8).

• You can choose to enter source information at the bottom of each Genealogy Report (see Chapter 8) by selecting **Options** from the **Contents** menu, and clicking the appropriate **Source Information** radio buttons.

7

Using Family Tree Maker's Scrapbook

You can add images to your Family File to link to individuals and to enhance charts, reports, and more. Family Tree Maker helps you organize your images into scrapbooks for each individual. In this chapter, you'll learn how to:

- Add images and other multimedia items
- Enter information about scrapbook items
- Rearrange scrapbook objects
- Enhance images
- Share your scrapbook

Each individual and each marriage in your Family File has a Scrapbook in which you can store photographs, documents, video, sound files, and other multimedia files. You can view these images in Scrapbook separately, or as a slide show, or you can use these images to enhance charts, reports, and other areas of Family Tree Maker. To use individual images in charts and the family group sheet, it is necessary to have the picture in the person's scrapbook.

NOTE

When you insert a picture or other object into a Family Tree Maker scrapbook, the original is not moved from its location. You should always maintain that original picture or multimedia file in case you wish to use it outside of Family Tree Maker. Multimedia objects are embedded into your family file and cannot be retrieved as separate files.

To access a scrapbook:

1. Go to the Family View of the individual or marriage.

2. Click the **Scrapbook** button next to the individual or marriage. The scrapbook window will appear.

TIP

You can access the Scrapbook page from other windows, including charts, reports, and Pedigree View, without returning to Family View. Click to select the individual, then click **Individual Scrapbook** or **Marriage Scrapbook** from the View menu. If the menu item is gray, the scrapbook is not available in that window.

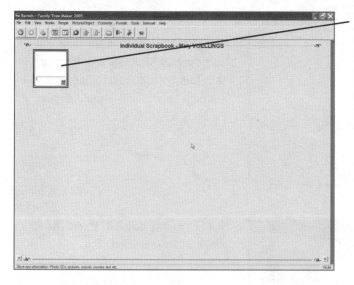

The empty, numbered frame in your scrapbook represents where the first image will go. Every time you fill in one frame with an image, a new blank frame will appear. Each frame can hold an image, sound clip, or another object.

Adding Images and Other Multimedia Objects

Adding Images

The easiest way to save an image to your Scrapbook is from a disc or from a location on your computer. You can also insert a picture from a scanner, digital camera, or photo CD.

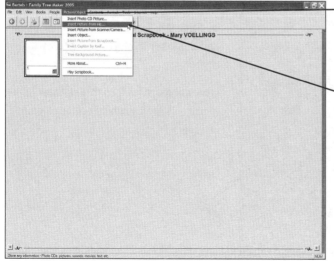

1. Click on the **Picture/Object** menu from the Scrapbook page you want to associate with the image. The Picture/Object menu will open.

2. Click on **Insert Photo CD Picture** or **Insert Picture from File**, depending on where you have your picture stored. The Insert Picture dialog box will open.

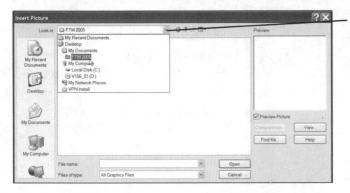

3. Click on the **Look in** drop-down arrow to locate the folder where you have saved your images. When you have found the correct folder, click on it, and the picture file should appear in the list box.

4. Click on the desired image. The image will be selected.

> ### NOTE
>
> You can preview the image you have selected in the Preview window of the Insert Picture dialog box.

5. Click **Open**. An Edit Picture dialog box will open with a view of the picture.

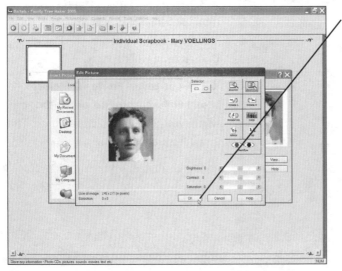

6. Click **OK**. The Edit Picture dialog box and the Insert Picture dialog box will close.

(You will learn later in this chapter how to use this dialog box to enhance your picture.)

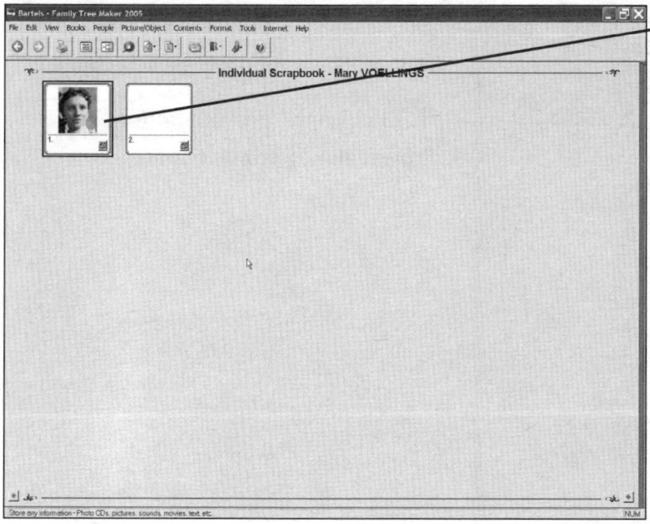

7. Your image will appear in the frame, which means it has been properly saved to Family Tree Maker's scrapbook.

TIP

You can also scan the picture directly into the scrapbook. From the **Picture/Object** menu, select **Insert Picture from Scanner/Camera**. Images can take up a lot of file space, so you may want to set your resolution to a maximum of 200 dpi (dots per inch). At this resolution, the image size will be large on your computer screen, but it will be blurry if you try to print it.

Saving Sound and Video Clips

You can save sound and video clips to your scrapbook similarly to how you saved an image.

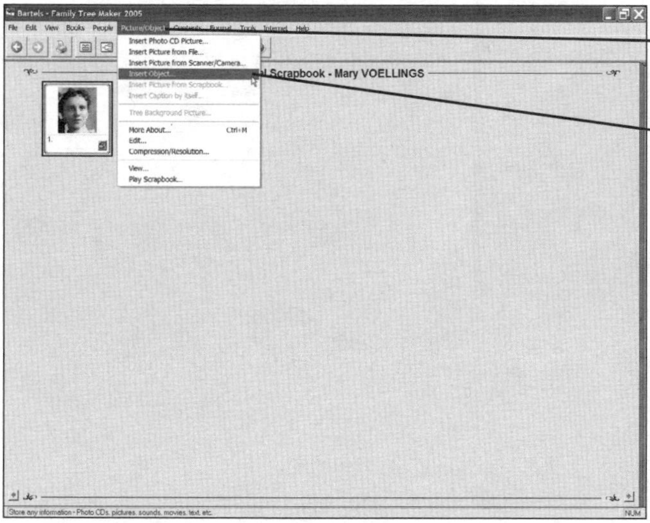

1. Click on **Picture/Object**. The Picture/Object menu will appear.

2. Click on **Insert Object**. The Insert Object dialog box will open.

3. Click on the **Create from File** radio button. The option will be selected.

4. Click on the **Browse** button. The Browse dialog box will open.

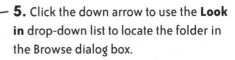

5. Click the down arrow to use the **Look in** drop-down list to locate the folder in the Browse dialog box.

6. Click on the desired file. The file will be selected.

7. Click on **Open**. The Browse dialog box will close. You will be returned to the Insert Object dialog box.

8. In the Insert Object dialog box, click on the **Display as Icon** check box. The option will be selected.

9. Click on **OK**. The Insert Object dialog box will close.

Using OLE Objects

Object Linking and Embedding (OLE) allows you to launch another program from within Family Tree Maker. You might want to do this so you can open a word-processing file to display a detailed family story.

1. Click **Insert Object** from the **Picture/Object** menu. The Insert Object dialog box will open.

2. Click on the **Create from File** radio button. The option will be selected.

> **TIP**
>
> If you click on the **Create New** radio button, you can select an object type from the list that appears. Then click on **OK** and the program will start if it is installed on your computer.

3. Click on the **Browse** button. The Browse dialog box will open.

4. Click the **Look in** drop-down arrow to select the desired folder.

5. Click on the desired file. The file will be selected.

6. Click on **Open**. The Browse dialog box will close. You will be returned to the Insert Object dialog box.

7. Click on the **Display as Icon** check box if you wish to display the object as an icon rather than showing the image of the object. You can also change the appearance of the icon by clicking **Change Icon**. Family Tree Maker will insert an icon in the scrapbook.

8. Click on **OK**. The Insert Object dialog box will close.

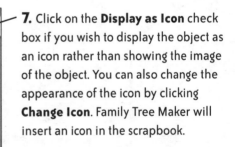

NOTE

Displaying an object as an icon makes it easier to identify multimedia objects such as sound and video files. The object will behave the same way whether or not you choose to display it as an icon.

TIP

When you save images to your scrapbook, the **Scrapbook** button in Family View changes to show that Scrapbook items have been added for the individual. First, a black triangle will appear in the bottom right corner of the button. Second, a number in parentheses following the word **Scrapbook** will indicate the number of images or objects added to the scrapbook page.

Entering Information about Scrapbook Objects

You can include a caption at the bottom of each frame.

1. Click on the **More About** button for the selected scrapbook item. The More About Picture/Object dialog box will open.

2. Type a caption in the **Caption** field.

3. Type a category in the **Category** field.

TIP

Plan ahead before you use the Category field. Family Tree Maker allows you to categorize your scrapbook objects, making them easier to search and add to charts. For example, you may want to name a category for events (e.g., weddings), or a time frame (e.g., baby photos), or a photo type (e.g., portraits).

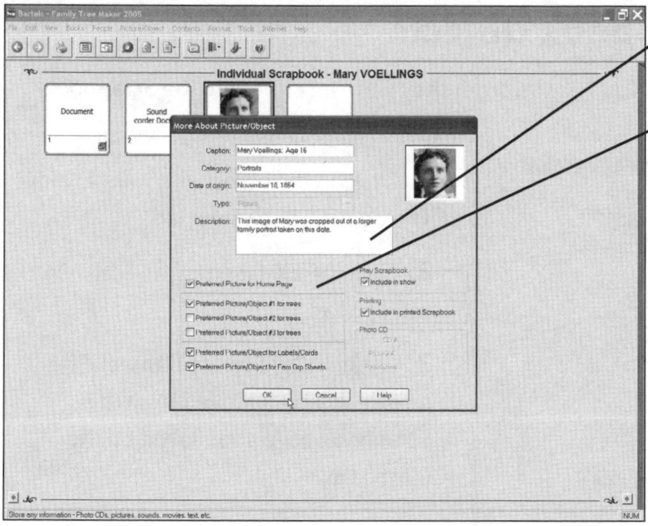

4. Type a description for the object in the **Description** field.

5. Click the check box(es) for your preferred selections. These options allow you to determine which images appear in charts, family group sheets, labels, and your home page. For example, if you select **Preferred Picture/Object #1** for trees and then create a tree chart using pictures designated as Preferred Picture/Object #1 for trees, this picture will appear next to the person in the chart. See Chapter 8 for more information on creating tree charts.

> **NOTE**
>
> Remember that only images will print, not sounds, video, and OLE objects.

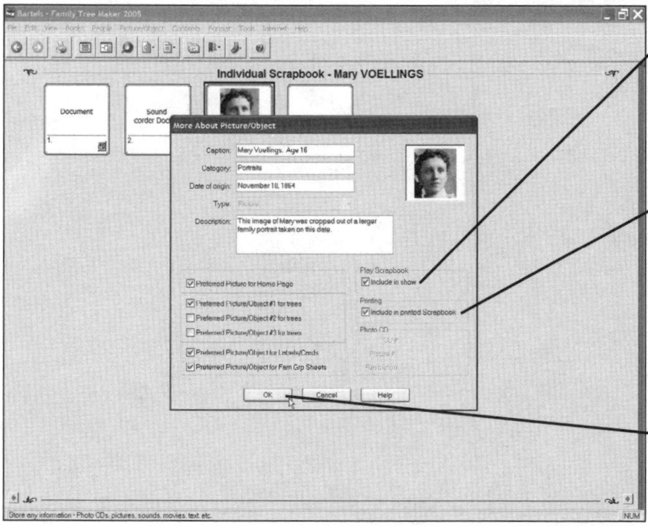

6. Click on the **Include in show** check box for objects you want to display when you play the scrapbook as a slideshow.

7. Click on the **Include in printed Scrapbook** check box if you want the object to be printed when you print the scrapbook. You may not want to include multimedia objects such as sound files since they will only print as icons.

8. Click on **OK**. The More About Picture/Object dialog box will close.

Rearranging Scrapbook Objects

Although images and objects display in the order they were inserted into the Scrapbook, you can rearrange the order.

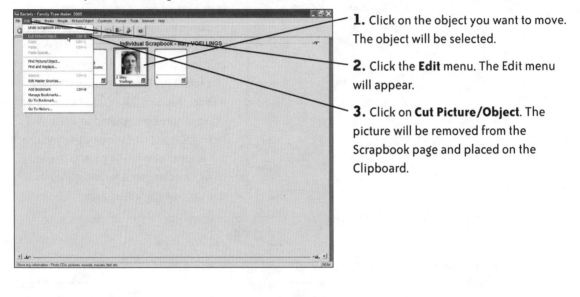

1. Click on the object you want to move. The object will be selected.

2. Click the **Edit** menu. The Edit menu will appear.

3. Click on **Cut Picture/Object**. The picture will be removed from the Scrapbook page and placed on the Clipboard.

4. Click on the frame where you want to place the object.

5. Click on **Edit**. The Edit menu will appear.

6. Click on **Paste Picture/Object**.

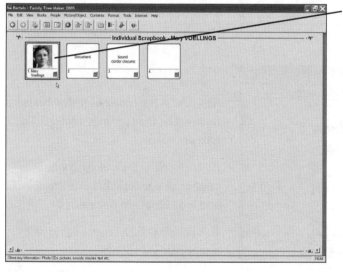

7. The object will be pasted in the new position and the object you have displaced will move one space to the right.

Copying Objects into Other Scrapbooks

You can copy a scrapbook item from the scrapbook of one individual to that of another individual.

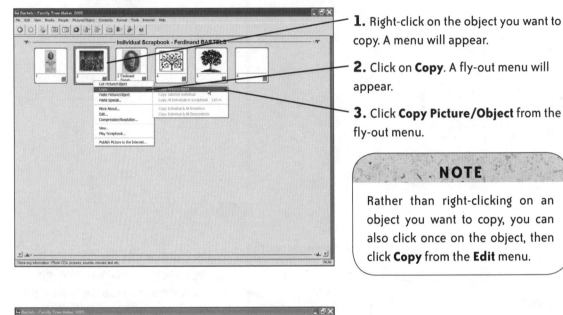

1. Right-click on the object you want to copy. A menu will appear.

2. Click on **Copy**. A fly-out menu will appear.

3. Click **Copy Picture/Object** from the fly-out menu.

NOTE

Rather than right-clicking on an object you want to copy, you can also click once on the object, then click **Copy** from the **Edit** menu.

4. Click on the **Index of Individuals** button. The Index of Individuals dialog box will open.

5. Click on the individual in whose scrapbook you want to paste the object. The individual will be selected.

6. Click on **OK**. The new individual's scrapbook will open.

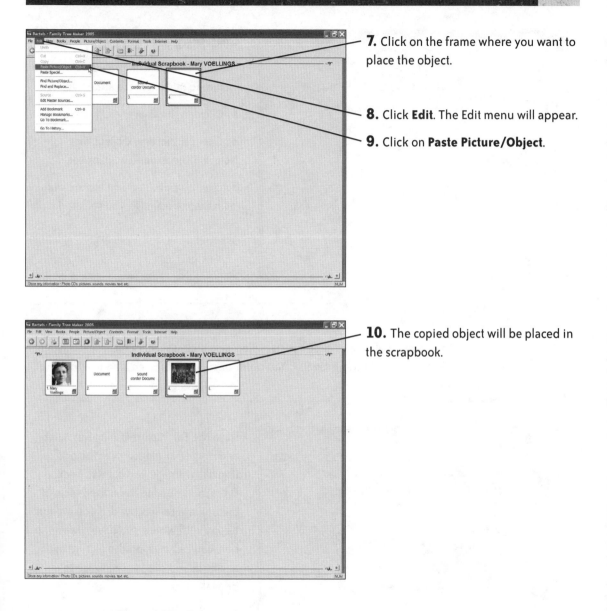

7. Click on the frame where you want to place the object.

8. Click **Edit**. The Edit menu will appear.

9. Click on **Paste Picture/Object**.

10. The copied object will be placed in the scrapbook.

Enhancing Images

As mentioned earlier in this chapter, you can enhance images that you add to your scrapbook. Using features built into Family Tree Maker you can rotate, crop, mirror, flip images, and adjust color, brightness, and remove red eye.

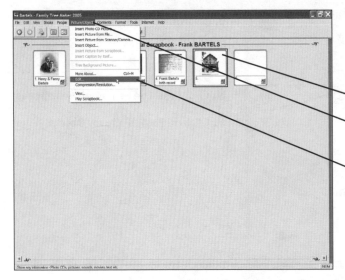

Cropping an Image

You may want to trim the edges of your picture to make it more attractive.

1. Click on the image you wish to crop.

2. Click on **Picture/Object**. The Picture/Object menu will appear.

3. Click on **Edit**. The Edit Picture dialog box for the image you selected will open.

TIP

This is the same dialog box that opens when you first save an image into your Scrapbook. You can edit the image at that point or reopen it for editing like you are doing now.

4. In the Edit Picture dialog box, click and drag your mouse over the portion of the image you want to keep. Everything outside the dotted lines of the box will be removed. If you are not happy with where you have drawn the box, you can click on the picture again, and click and drag your mouse to redraw the box.

5. Click on the **Crop** button. The picture will be cropped.

6. Click **OK** to save your changes or **Cancel** to close the dialog box without saving any changes.

Adjusting the Color and Brightness of the Image

You may be able to enhance your picture by lightening or darkening it. For example, you might want to darken an old photo that has faded to see if it will bring out some of the details in the image.

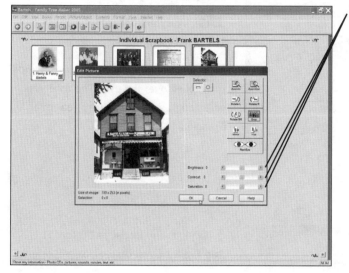

The brightness, contrast, and saturation tools are in the bottom right-hand corner of the Edit Picture dialog box. To make changes to the image, click on the right or left arrow for each tool or drag the square in the middle to the left or right with your mouse.

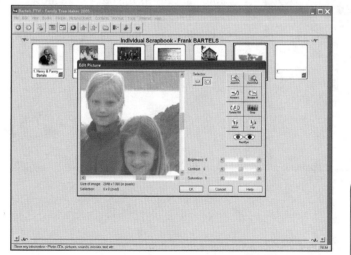

Correcting Red Eye

Use this feature to correct the red-eye effect that may have occurred in your photographs.

1. Go to the individual's Edit Picture dialog box, by following steps 1-3 from the previous section.

> **TIP**
>
> You can also go to an individual's Edit Picture dialog box by right-clicking on the picture and selecting **Edit** from the menu that appears.

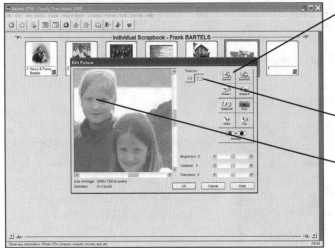

2. In the Edit Picture dialog box, click on the **Zoom In** button as many times as you need to in order to bring the eyes into a close focus. Slide the scroll bar if necessary until the eyes come into view.

3. Click on the **oval selector** button. The oval button will be selected.

4. Select the area of the eye by dragging the mouse over the eye. The oval you selected in step four will appear over the eye.

5. Click on the **Red-Eye** button. The Red Eye Removal dialog box will open.

6. Click **OK** to let Family Tree Maker automatically fix the red eye. In most cases, you will not need to make any adjustments to the image yourself.

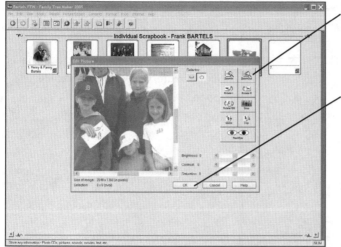

7. Zoom back out to see the effect. If you are not satisfied with the results, you can manually adjust the colors using the controls.

8. Once you are satisfied with your changes, click on **OK** to close the dialog box.

Searching for Scrapbook Objects

You may reach a point where you have so many objects stored in your Scrapbook that you have difficulty finding a particular file quickly. You can use the Find feature to speed your search.

1. Go to the individual's Scrapbook page (by using the **Scrapbook** button or **View** menu as you learned at the beginning of this chapter).

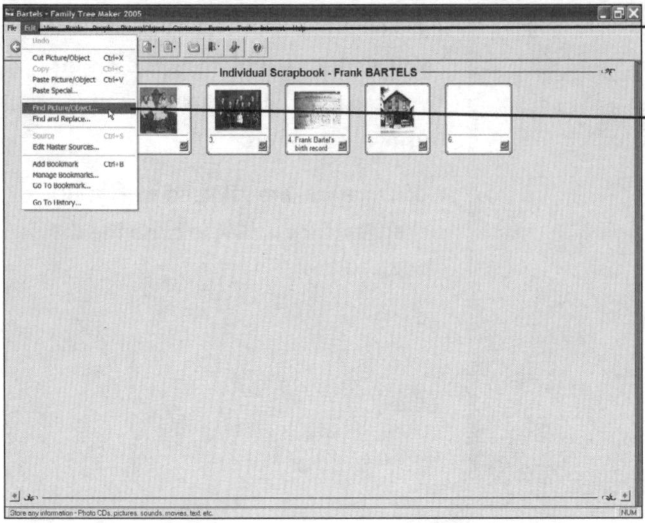

2. Click on the **Edit**. The edit menu will appear.

3. Click on **Find Picture/Object**. The Find Picture/Object dialog box will open.

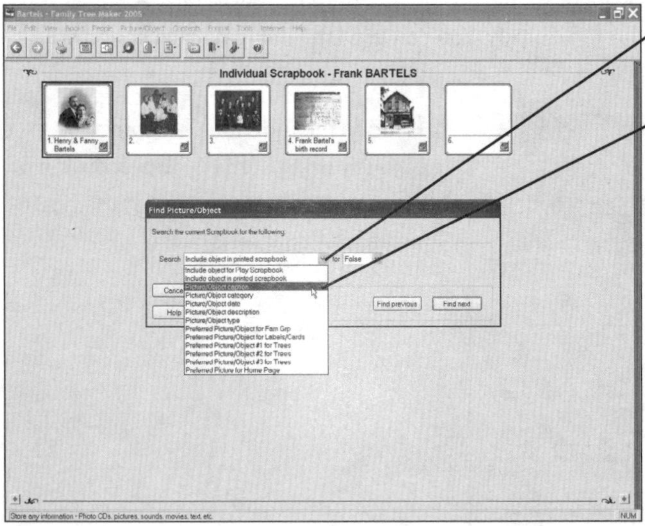

4. Click on the **Search down** arrow. The Search drop-down list will appear.

5. Click the search item you want to use. The option will be selected.

TIP

If you are searching for a regular image in your program, you will probably want to choose Picture/ Object type in the Search box and Picture in the second box. Another common choice is to search on the Picture/Object caption field, for a word you have typed into the caption.

6. In the **for** field, type the term for which you want to search.

7. Click on the **Find next** button. The dialog box will stay up, but Family Tree Maker will highlight the first frame that matches that description.

8. If Family Tree Maker finds the object you are seeking, click **Cancel** in the Find Picture/Object dialog box to close the dialog box. If not, click **Find next** to search for the next possible match.

Sharing Your Scrapbook

You can display your scrapbook in a slideshow on your computer. If you have recorded sound into your scrapbook, you can listen to that as well, if you have speakers on your computer.

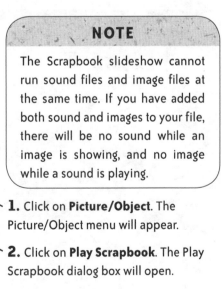

NOTE

The Scrapbook slideshow cannot run sound files and image files at the same time. If you have added both sound and images to your file, there will be no sound while an image is showing, and no image while a sound is playing.

1. Click on **Picture/Object**. The Picture/Object menu will appear.

2. Click on **Play Scrapbook**. The Play Scrapbook dialog box will open.

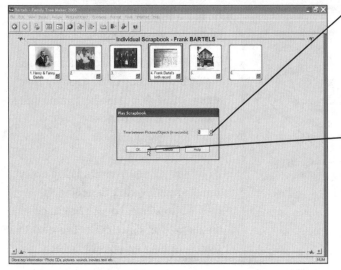

3. Click the **up** and **down arrows** to increase and decrease the delay between objects in the scrapbook. Or, highlight the number in the field and type a new number over the existing number.

4. Click on **OK**. The scrapbook will be played.

Printing Scrapbook Pages

To print a scrapbook page, make sure you are in the individual's scrapbook page, and have the printer turned on.

1. Click the **Print** button. The Print Scrapbook dialog box will open.

2. Click **OK** in the Print Scrapbook dialog box. The dialog box will close and the scrapbook images and captions will print.

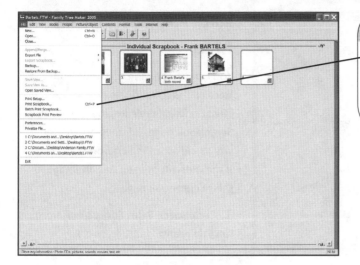

NOTE

You can also open the Print Scrapbook dialog box by selecting **Print Scrapbook** from the **File** menu.

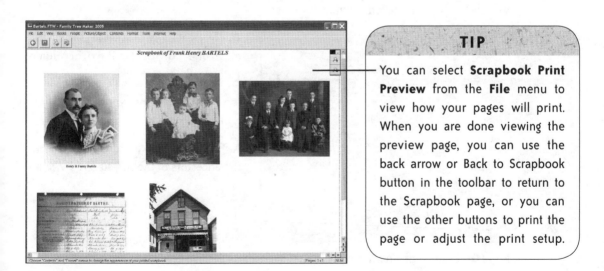

TIP

You can select **Scrapbook Print Preview** from the **File** menu to view how your pages will print. When you are done viewing the preview page, you can use the back arrow or Back to Scrapbook button in the toolbar to return to the Scrapbook page, or you can use the other buttons to print the page or adjust the print setup.

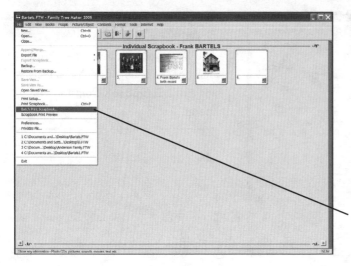

Batch Printing Scrapbook Pages

You can print all the scrapbook images from all the individuals in your Family File at once. Make sure you are in a Scrapbook page – it does not matter which individual's Scrapbook page, or if the individual even has an image in their Scrapbook page.

1. Click **Batch Print Scrapbook** from the **File** menu.

2. The Individuals to Include in Batch Print dialog box will appear. Select which individuals' scrapbook pages you want to print by moving them to the column on the right. To do this, click a name in the left column, then press:

a. The right angle bracket (>) button to move one individual to the right column

b. The right double angle bracket button (>>) to move everyone over to the right column

c. The Ancestors> button to move all the ancestors of the selected individuals

d. Etc.

3. When you are done, press **OK**. The Batch Print Scrapbook page will appear. Press **OK** again to begin printing.

You will learn how to use your scrapbook images in charts, reports, and on your personal Internet Home page, in the following chapters of this book.

PART

III

Creating and Printing Charts and Reports

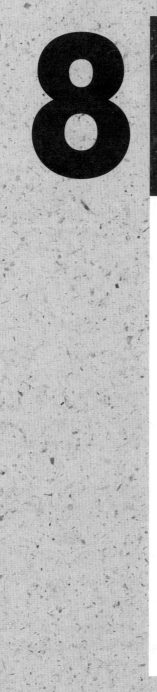

Creating Tree Charts and Printing

After you have entered information about your family into Family Tree Maker, you will likely want to display the information in a tree, chart, or graph. Family Tree Maker offers a number of different trees that will show your ancestors, descendants, or both for a selected individual. In this chapter, you'll learn how to:

- Select the tree you want to print
- Customize and format a chart
- Add photographs and images to charts
- Print charts
- Save the chart in PDF format

In Chapter 2, you learned how to display the different tree charts in Family Tree Maker. You can customize these charts. The method for printing tree charts applies to reports and other areas of Family Tree Maker as well, including Scrapbooks.

Viewing the Tree You Want to Print

1. Click on the **tree charts** button in the toolbar. A drop-down menu will appear.

2. Click on the tree you want to display from the drop-down menu.

Here's a quick review of each of the tree types you opened in Chapter 2.

• **Standard Pedigree Tree** – Displays direct line ancestors of an individual, with blank spaces showing for ancestors where details have been left out. This is the standard tree among genealogists.

• **Ancestor Tree** – Standard, Fan, and Vertical – Displays direct line ancestors of an individual. This chart uses boxes rather than the plain lines of the standard pedigree tree, and allows for more personalization.

• **Descendant Tree** - Standard, Fan – Displays descendants of an individual.

• **Hourglass Tree** - Standard, Fan – Displays both ancestors and descendants of an individual with ancestors above and descendants below in a shape similar to the hourglass.

• **All-in-One Tree** – Displays every individual that has been entered into the Family File. You can click on the Options button to select if you want to show unconnected step-family trees and/or unrelated trees.

Customizing and Formatting a Chart

You can change the amount of information that is displayed in the tree, as well as text style, box shape, size, background color, and borders of the chart. You can also use templates to change the overall appearance of a tree.

Changing the Number of Generations in a Chart

You can decide how many generations you want to appear in your chart.

Contents	Format	Tools	Internet
Items to Include in each Box...			
Individuals to Include...			
Title & Footnote...			
# of Generations to Show...			
Options...			

1. Click the **tree chart** button and select a chart.

2. Click **# of Generations to Show** from the **Contents menu**. The # of Generations to Show dialog box will open.

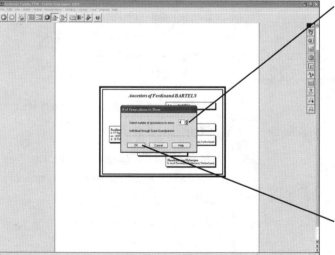

3. Click the **up** and **down** arrows to select the number of generations you would like to appear in your chart.

TIP

Instead of using the up and down arrows to select the number of generations, you can also highlight the number and type in a new number over the highlighted number.

4. Click **OK**. The dialog box will close and the chart will change to show no more than the number of generations you have selected.

Using the Format Button

Family Tree Maker allows you to change the format of the chart. For example, a fan chart can show the ancestors in a semi-circle around the root individual, or in a complete circle around the root individual. The Format button options differ between the Fan and Pedigree Charts because of the differences between the types of charts.

Using the Format Button in a Fan chart:

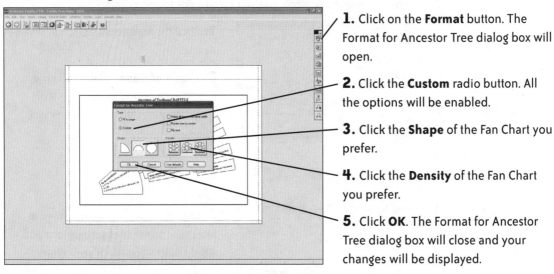

1. Click on the **Format** button. The Format for Ancestor Tree dialog box will open.

2. Click the **Custom** radio button. All the options will be enabled.

3. Click the **Shape** of the Fan Chart you prefer.

4. Click the **Density** of the Fan Chart you prefer.

5. Click **OK**. The Format for Ancestor Tree dialog box will close and your changes will be displayed.

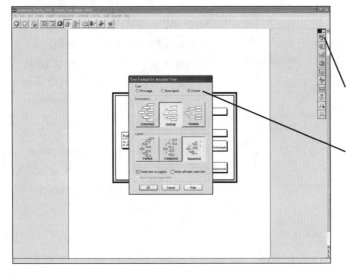

Using the Format Button in Standard tree:

1. Click on the **Format** button. The Tree Format for Ancestor Tree dialog box will open.

2. Click the **Type** of Ancestor Tree you want to display.

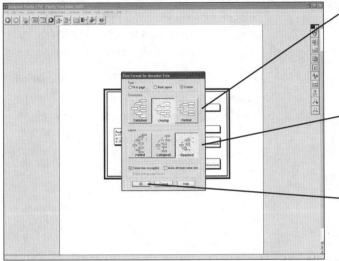

3. Click the **Connections** you want to use in the chart. The chart's boxes will be moved closer together or farther apart, depending on the type of connections you select.

4. Click **Custom** to activate buttons if you want to change the **Layout**, then click on the type of layout you would like to see.

5. Click on **OK**. The Tree Format for Ancestor Tree dialog box will close and your changes will be displayed.

TIP

When you select the Book layout or custom type, you can elect to have each tree centered on the page.

TIP

Click on the **Zoom Out** button to see more of the tree. Click on the **Zoom In** button for a larger view of a portion of the tree.

Rearranging the Standard Ancestor Chart

If you do not like where Family Tree Maker has placed an individual on a pedigree chart, you can move the individual box for that person or a complete lineage, using your mouse and the keyboard. This can only be done in standard ancestor and standard descendant trees.

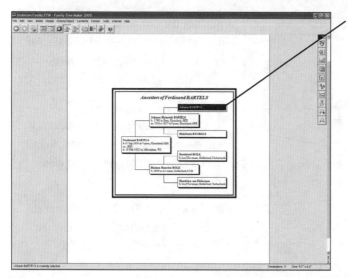

1. Click on the individual whose lineage you want to move. The individual and his or her lineage are selected.

2. Drag the mouse to the new location. The individual or the selected lineage will be moved elsewhere on the chart.

NOTE

Remember that when you are dragging the mouse, you need to hold down the left mouse button or the left mouse button and the Ctrl key while you are dragging the lineage or individual to a new location.

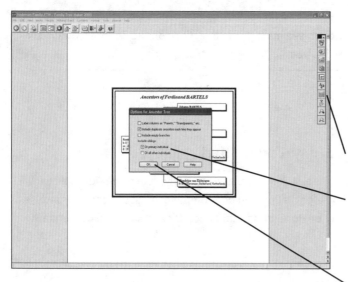

Including Siblings on Trees

You can use any of the Ancestor Tree formats or the Standard Hourglass Tree to add siblings to your tree.

1. Click the **tree chart** button and click a chart.

2. Click the **Options** button. The Options for Tree dialog box will open.

3. Click the **Include siblings** check box for the siblings you wish to add to the tree. A check mark will appear in the selected box.

4. Click **OK**. The Options for Tree dialog box will close.

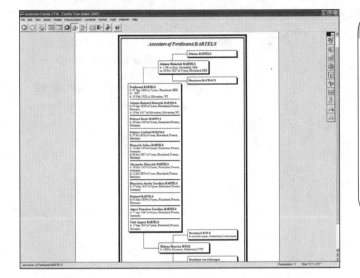

NOTE

Notice how the changes affect the overall look of the Ancestor Tree, especially if you have elected to include the siblings for everyone on the tree. Even when you select this option, the siblings will be left out if there is not enough space for them when you print, unless you have chosen a custom layout.

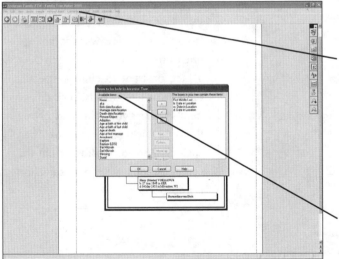

Including and Excluding Items in Tree Chart

1. Click **Items to Include in Each Box** from the **Contents** menu. The Items to Include in Tree dialog box will appear. The items listed in the box on the right are the items that will appear in the tree, while the items in the box on the left are the items you can select to include in the tree.

2. Click on the item in the **Available items** box to add items you want to include in your tree chart. Then, click on the arrow pointing to the right. A dialog box containing options for that item will appear.

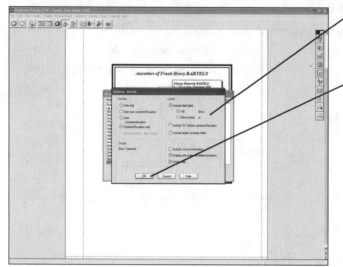

3. Click the radio buttons and check mark boxes to select which facts you would like to include in the chart.

4. Click **OK**. The dialog box will close and the fact will be added to the boxes in your tree.

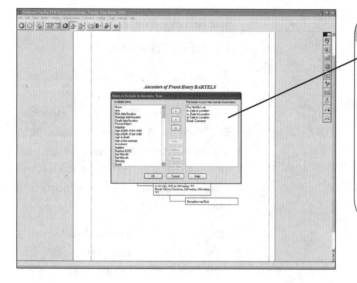

TIP

If you decide you want to change one of the options you selected for a fact, or want to change specific options or font details, click on the item in the right-hand box of the Items to Include dialog box, then click on **Font** or **Options** from the center buttons, whichever selection is appropriate.

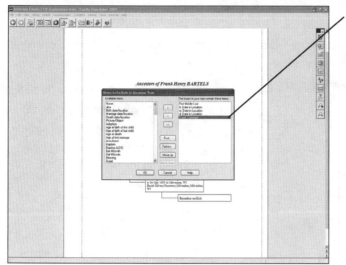

5. To move items out of the box on the right and back to the box on the left, click on the item, then click on the left arrow.

TIP

Use the double left arrows to remove all items from the right box to the left box at once.

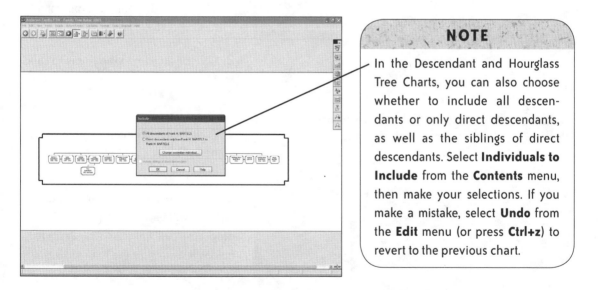

NOTE

In the Descendant and Hourglass Tree Charts, you can also choose whether to include all descendants or only direct descendants, as well as the siblings of direct descendants. Select **Individuals to Include** from the **Contents** menu, then make your selections. If you make a mistake, select **Undo** from the **Edit** menu (or press **Ctrl+z**) to revert to the previous chart.

NOTE

You can add titles and footnotes to your tree chart. From the **Contents** menu, select **Title & Footnote**. The Title and Footnote Tree dialog box will appear. Type in the information and then press **OK**. Your footnote will be included.

Customizing Font

You can change the appearance of the words in your chart to make them appear more formal, or more fun, etc., by selecting a different font.

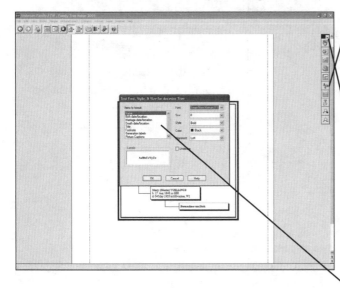

1. Click on the **Text Font, Style, & Size** button in the vertical toolbar. The Text Font, Style, & Size dialog box will appear. The complete name of the dialog box will depend on the tree or report that you have selected.

NOTE

When you print the chart, the vertical toolbar will not be printed. You can click on the minimizing button at the top of the toolbar to minimize the vertical toolbar.

2. Click on an item in the **Items to format** list.

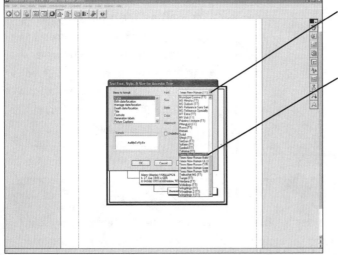

3. Click on the down arrow to the right of the **Font** field. The font drop-down list will appear.

4. Click on the font you want to use. The font will be selected and the Font drop-down list will close. The **Sample** field will show how the font you have selected will appear in the chart.

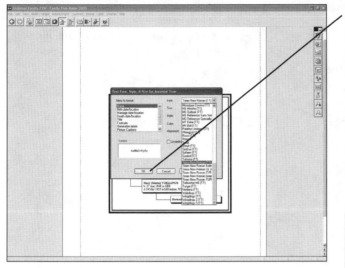

5. Click **OK** if you like the way the font looks in the Sample field, and any other selections you have made. You can also change the size of the text (font size), style, color, and alignment in the same way you changed the font. The Text Font, Style, & Size dialog box will close and the changes to the font will be displayed.

> **TIP**
>
> You can see a sample of each font in the Sample box by using the keyboard arrows to move through the list of fonts.

Boxes, Borders, Lines, and Background Color

You can beautify and personalize your tree charts by changing the box styles, borders, and background colors of your tree.

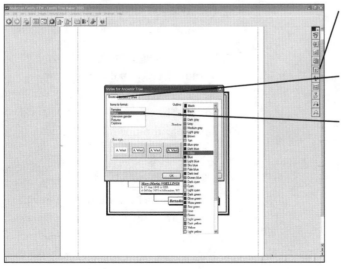

1. Click on the **Box, Line & Border Styles** button. The Styles for Tree dialog box will open.

2. Click on the **Boxes** tab if the dialog box does not already default to this tab.

3. Click to select an item for which you want to apply a format in the **Items to format** box.

> **TIP**
>
> You can also hold down the **Ctrl** key and click on each item to select more than one item at a time.

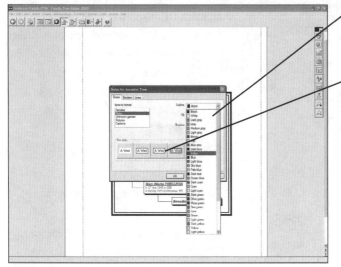

4. Click the drop-down menus to select the colors for the outline, fill, and shadow.

5. Click to select a box style.

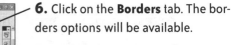

6. Click on the **Borders** tab. The borders options will be available.

7. Click on the desired **Border style**. The first style indicates no border at all. The style you select will appear to be indented to show it has been selected.

8. Click on the drop-down arrow for **Border** color. From the drop-down menu, select the color you want for your border. The color will be selected and the color drop-down list will close.

> **NOTE**
>
> If you select the border style with no border, the border color will not show.

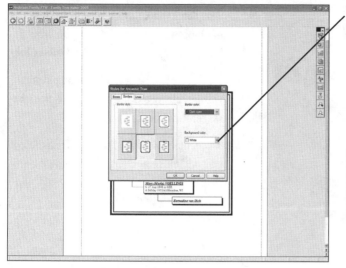

9. Click on the drop-down arrow for **Background** color. The Background color list will appear. Click on the color you want for your background. The color will be selected and the color drop-down list will close.

TIP

Choose None for your background color if you do not want to print a color background.

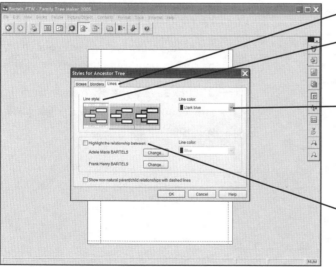

10. Click on the **Lines** tab.

11. Click on the desired **Line style**. The style you select will be indented to show it has been selected.

12. Click on the drop-down arrow for **Line color**. From the drop-down menu, select the color you want for your border. The color will be selected and the color drop-down list will close.

13. Click the **Highlight the relation-ship between** check box if you want to emphasize the relationship between two individuals in your tree.

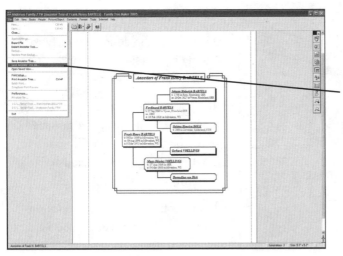

14. Click the **Change** button to select each of the two individuals you would like to compare, and select a **Line color**.

15. Click the bottom check box if you want to show a dotted line for non-natural relationships.

16. Click **OK**. The Styles for Tree dialog box will close and the changes will be displayed.

Save Your Chart

Now that you've customized your chart, be sure to save your changes.

1. Click **Save [type of] Tree As** from the **File** menu. The Save View as dialog box will open.

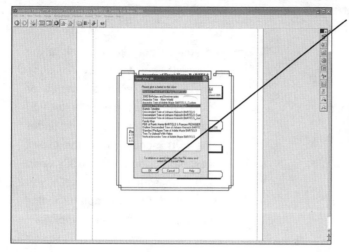

2. Type a name for your new tree, then press **OK**. You have now saved the changes to your tree.

> ### NOTE
>
> To open a saved tree, click **Open Saved View** from the **File** menu.

Templates

Family Tree Maker has several templates you can choose from with creative borders and other artwork.

> ### NOTE
>
> If you have spent a lot of time customizing a tree chart, make sure to save your customized chart before using templates so you do not lose your work.

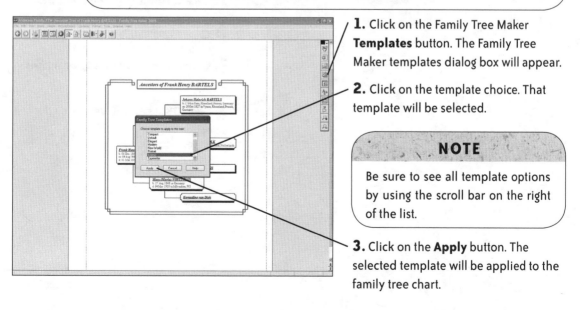

1. Click on the Family Tree Maker **Templates** button. The Family Tree Maker templates dialog box will appear.

2. Click on the template choice. That template will be selected.

> ### NOTE
>
> Be sure to see all template options by using the scroll bar on the right of the list.

3. Click on the **Apply** button. The selected template will be applied to the family tree chart.

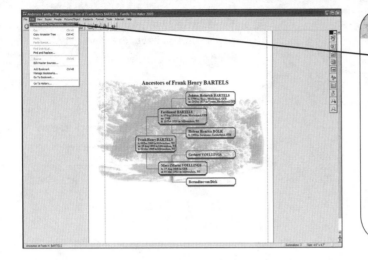

If you do not like the look of the template, and you have not done anything else, such as zooming in or out to view the template better, you can use the **Undo** command under the **Edit** menu item or the **Ctrl+z** keyboard shortcut to quickly undo the changes to the reports. Or, you can return to the Templates dialog box to select a different template.

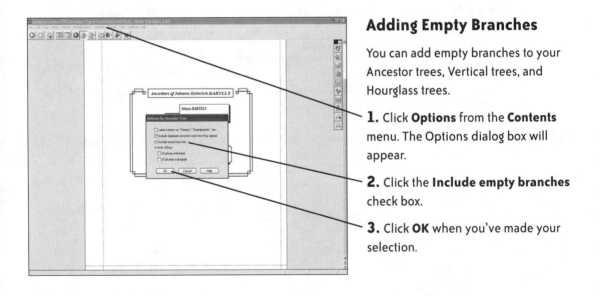

Adding Empty Branches

You can add empty branches to your Ancestor trees, Vertical trees, and Hourglass trees.

1. Click **Options** from the **Contents** menu. The Options dialog box will appear.

2. Click the **Include empty branches** check box.

3. Click **OK** when you've made your selection.

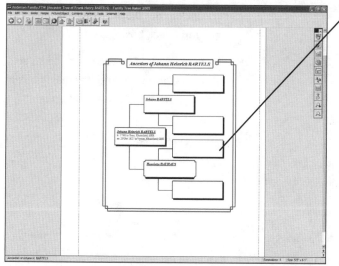

4. The dialog box will close and the tree will change to show the empty branches.

Adding Photographs and Images to Charts

You can include background images in any of your Tree Charts. You can also add individual photographs to family group sheets within the boxes of any of the tree charts except for the fan charts. To add a background image to a tree chart, the file must be somewhere on your computer. However, to add an individual picture to a family group sheet or tree chart, the photograph must have already been added to the scrapbook area (See Chapter 7) of your Family File, for the individuals included in the chart.

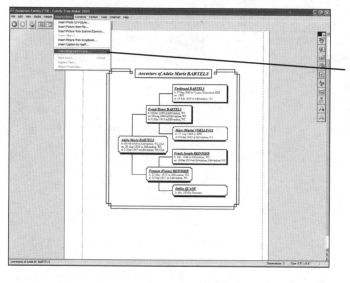

To add a background image:

1. Open a tree chart.

2. Click **Tree Background Picture** from the **Picture/Object** menu. A Background Picture dialog box will appear.

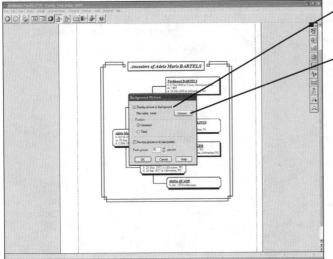

3. Click in the **Display picture in back-ground** check box.

4. Click on the **Choose** button to select an image or photo. Another dialog box with a list of directories will appear.

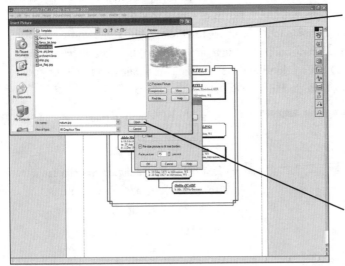

5. Click the **Look-in** drop down arrow if your photograph or image is not located in the default directory. You can switch to a different directory.

TIP

You can preview the image if the Preview Picture checkbox is checked.

6. Click **Open** when you have selected the desired photograph or image. The Edit Picture dialog box will appear.

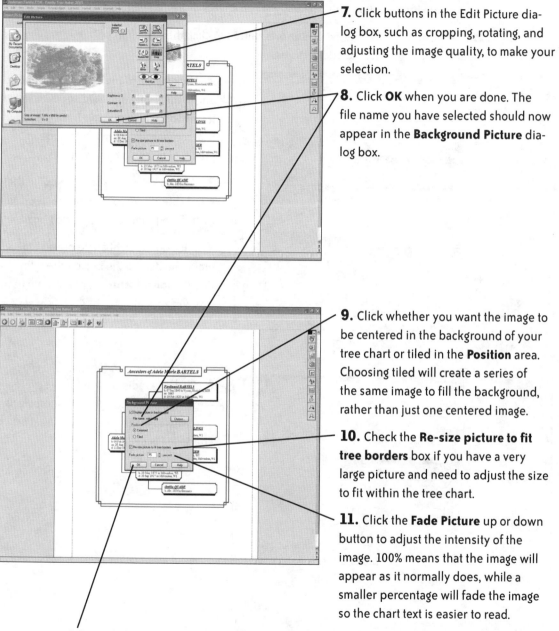

7. Click buttons in the Edit Picture dialog box, such as cropping, rotating, and adjusting the image quality, to make your selection.

8. Click **OK** when you are done. The file name you have selected should now appear in the **Background Picture** dialog box.

9. Click whether you want the image to be centered in the background of your tree chart or tiled in the **Position** area. Choosing tiled will create a series of the same image to fill the background, rather than just one centered image.

10. Check the **Re-size picture to fit tree borders** box if you have a very large picture and need to adjust the size to fit within the tree chart.

11. Click the **Fade Picture** up or down button to adjust the intensity of the image. 100% means that the image will appear as it normally does, while a smaller percentage will fade the image so the chart text is easier to read.

12. Click **OK** when you are done adjusting the image selection, position, and color intensity. The Background Picture dialog box will close and the image will display in the background.

To add individual photographs to family group sheets or tree charts:

1. Use the **Tree Charts** button or **Reports** button to click the tree chart or family group sheet in which you want to add pictures.

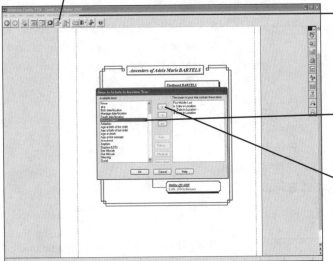

2. Click **Items to Include in each Box** under the **Contents** menu, or click the **Items to Include button** from the vertical toolbar. The Items to Include in [name of tree] dialog box opens.

3. Click to select **Picture/Object** in the **Available items** column of the Items to Include in [name of tree] dialog box.

4. Click on the right angle bracket to move the item to the box on the right. The **Options: Picture/Object** dialog box will appear.

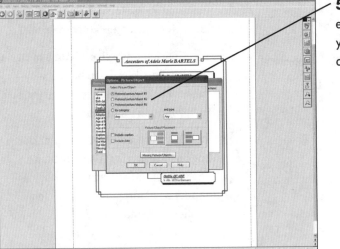

5. Click the radio button for the preference number or category of photograph you wish to add to the group sheet or chart.

> ### NOTE
>
> When you add a photograph to a scrapbook, you can assign a preferred number to the photograph. This allows you to choose which photographs you wish to include in different charts more quickly. For example, you may wish to always use a particular photograph of an individual for that person's family group sheet but a different photograph for a tree chart. When you create the chart, choose which set of preferred photographs to use. Similarly, you can opt to create categories of photographs (e.g., wedding, baby pictures, photos for pedigree charts) and use a category when adding photos to a chart. For more information on scrapbooks, see Chapter 7.

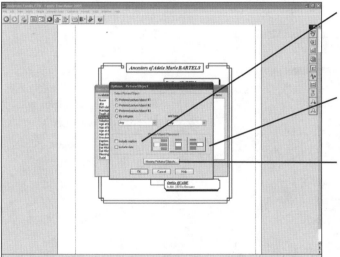

6. Click the check boxes if you wish to include the caption or date you attributed to the photograph when you added it to the scrapbook.

7. Click the button for how you want to position the text next to the photograph in the **Picture/Object Placement** box.

8. Click on the **Missing Pictures/ Objects** button if no picture exists in the scrapbook for the individual. The Missing Pictures/Objects dialog box will open.

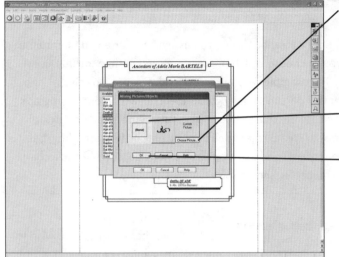

9. Click the image you want to put in the box if no picture exists in the scrapbook, or select a different image from a file anywhere on your computer by clicking on the **Choose Picture** button.

10. Click on **None** to leave the area blank if no picture exists.

11. Click **OK** to accept your Missing Pictures/Objects options. The Missing Pictures/Objects dialog box will close.

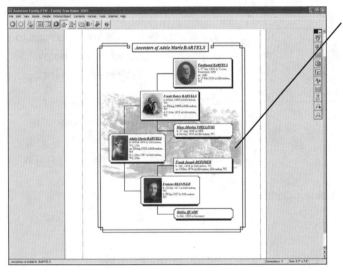

12. Click **OK** to accept the changes you made to the chart. The dialog box will close and the changes will appear in your chart.

Printing Charts

When you are done customizing your chart, you may want to print the chart. First, you will need to understand various aspects of print setup.

Dotted Lines

Depending on what tree chart you have open, you may have noticed dotted lines running vertically and horizontally across the page. These lines represent the margins of standard 8 ½" x 11" sheet of paper. If those dotted lines cross through a part of your tree, you may want to change the formatting to fit the tree on one page, or use the book layout option to include continuation indicators for multiple pages. You can also export a large tree to PDF format and have it printed on large paper by a copy/printing store. You can also tape pages together if you prefer to use your own printer.

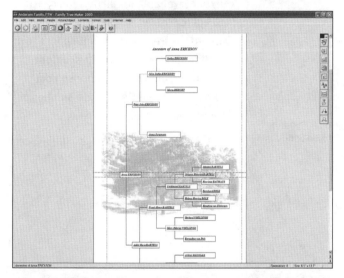

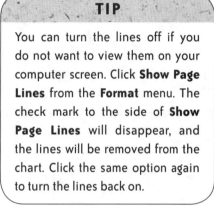

TIP

You can turn the lines off if you do not want to view them on your computer screen. Click **Show Page Lines** from the **Format** menu. The check mark to the side of **Show Page Lines** will disappear, and the lines will be removed from the chart. Click the same option again to turn the lines back on.

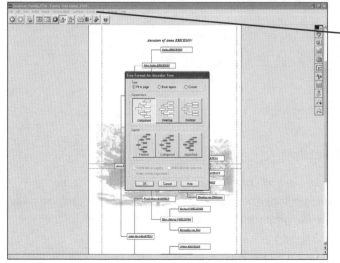

To format a Tree shape:

1. Click **Tree Format** from the **Format** menu. The Tree Format dialog box will open. The options available through this dialog box will vary depending on the type of tree you have selected.

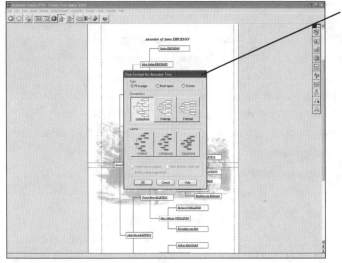

2. Click the formatting options you want for your tree. If you choose the **Fit to page** option but the number of individuals to show is too large to fit all of the desired information, Family Tree Maker will verify that you want it to modify the amount of information shown in order to fit the tree. The **book layout** (available for all non-fan charts except for the All-in-One tree) will spread the tree over multiple pages with continuation indicators. The **custom layout** will allow you to choose your own layout regardless of the number of pages the chart takes.

3. Click **OK**. The dialog box will close and the format will change.

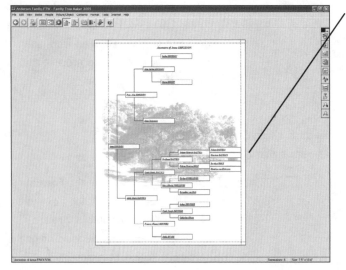

Using Options in Print Setup

You can make a tree shorter or narrower by changing the type of content on the tree; various ways to change content were mentioned above. You can also change margins and print orientation. Changes you make to the print setup will only change the settings for the type of chart with which you are working.

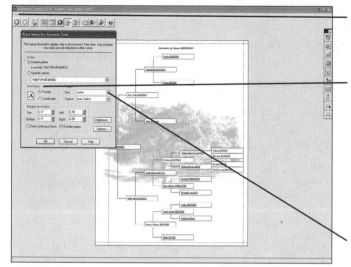

1. Click **Print setup** from the **File** menu. The Print Setup Tree dialog box will appear.

2. Click the **Portrait** option under **Orientation** if you want your document to print with the short edge of the paper at the bottom (the way a letter normally prints). This is the default setting. Click the **Landscape** option if you want your document to print with the long edge of the paper at the bottom.

3. Paper Size - Click the down arrow next to **Size** to change the size of the paper, if your printer is capable of printing larger sheets of paper. Otherwise, leave the selection at Letter size, which is a standard 8 ½" x 11" sheet of paper.

4. Margins (in inches) – Click the up and down arrows next to each margin to change the margin size on your page. By default, each page prints with 1" margins at the top, a quarter inch of margin on the left and right, and .17 inch margin at the bottom.

5. Print continuous forms box – Click this check box if you use an older printer with the continuous sheets on perforated paper, to have the chart print across the perforations. Click **Overlap pages** if you use a laser printer that feeds single sheets at a time.

6. Click **OK** to close the print setup dialog box and save your changes.

To Print:

1. Click **Print Tree** from the **File** menu. The menu item name will reflect the tree you have open, e.g., Print Descendant Tree.

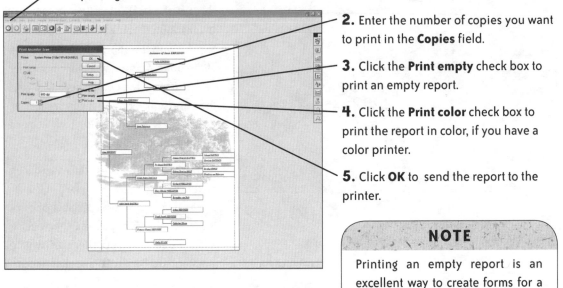

2. Enter the number of copies you want to print in the **Copies** field.

3. Click the **Print empty** check box to print an empty report.

4. Click the **Print color** check box to print the report in color, if you have a color printer.

5. Click **OK** to send the report to the printer.

> ### NOTE
>
> Printing an empty report is an excellent way to create forms for a research trip.

Saving the Chart in PDF Format

You can share your tree charts with others even if they do not own the Family Tree Maker program. Do this by using the Portable Document Format (PDF) that can be viewed using Adobe® Reader®, which is available as a free download from the Adobe website.

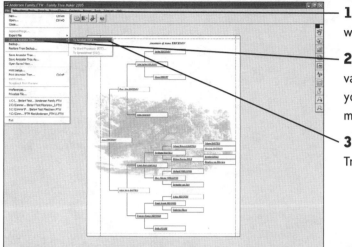

1. Click on the **File** menu. The File menu will appear.

2. Click **Export Tree.** (The name will vary slightly depending on which tree you have open.) Another drop-down menu will appear.

3. Click **To Acrobat (PDF)**. The Export Tree dialog box will open.

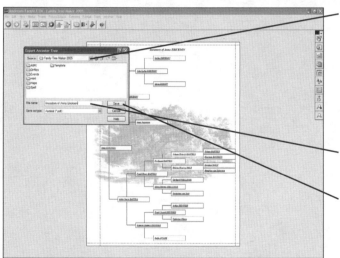

4. Click the **Save in** drop-down arrow to choose where you want to save your file, or use the Family Tree Maker default location. Be sure to make a note so you can find the file later. This is also a good time to save the PDF directly to a disk if you want to share your report with someone.

5. Type a new name in the **File name** field.

6. Click the **Save** button.

7. Click **OK** when you see a message reminding you that you need the Adobe Reader to view the file.

8. Click **OK** when you see a message telling you the export is complete.

9. If you did not choose to save the PDF to a disk in Step 4, you can do so now, or you can attach the PDF to an e-mail to send to others.

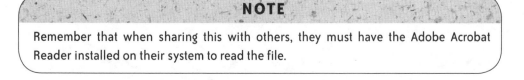

NOTE

Remember that when sharing this with others, they must have the Adobe Acrobat Reader installed on their system to read the file.

9

Creating Genealogy and Research Reports

You may want to share more in-depth reports with family members and fellow researchers. Genealogy and research reports are more detail-loaded and are the best format to use for this purpose. In this chapter, you'll learn how to:

- Select a genealogy style
- Format a report
- Create endnotes
- Create a bibliography
- Create a report of facts with sources
- Create a research journal

In Chapter 2, you learned how to display the different genealogy reports in Family Tree Maker. Genealogy reports in Family Tree Maker are generally narrative reports. This chapter covers three narrative-style reports, as well reports that are created specifically to keep track of research – end notes, bibliographies, and the Family Tree Maker Research Journal.

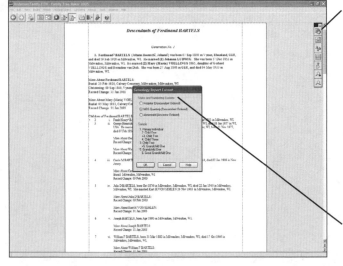

Selecting and Viewing Genealogy Reports

To display the report you want to customize or print:

1. Click on the **Report** button in the toolbar. A drop-down menu will appear.

2. Click on **Genealogy Report**. A Genealogy Report will open.

3. Click on the **Report Format** button on the vertical toolbar.

> ### NOTE
> Instead of clicking Report Format from the vertical toolbar, you can also click **Genealogy Report** format from the **Format** menu. The Genealogy Report Format dialog box will open.

4. Click on the **Style and number system** you would like to use.

Format Styles

The format styles are described below. In addition, the sample box in the Genealogy Report Format dialog box changes to show how each style would appear and be numbered.

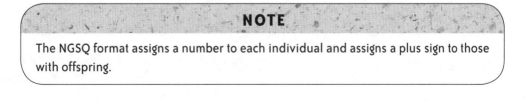

Using the Register Format

The Register format report is the format accepted by the New England Historic Genealogical Society, the oldest genealogical society in the United States. The Register format dates back to 1870 and is used to show someone's lineage. This report lists individuals and details about a family beginning with a particular ancestor and moving to descendants.

NOTE

The Register format assigns an identifying number to those who have offspring.

Using the NGSQ Format

Like the Register format, the NGS Quarterly format lists information about a family starting with an ancestor and moving forward in time to that individual's descendants. This is the preferred genealogical report of the National Genealogical Society. The format dates back to 1912.

NOTE

The NGSQ format assigns a number to each individual and assigns a plus sign to those with offspring.

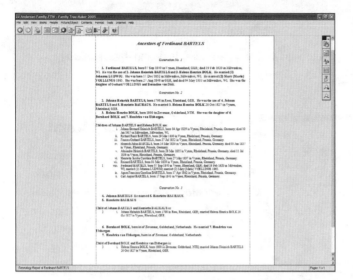

Using the Ahnentafel Report

The Ahnentafel format is ancestor-ordered, meaning that it starts with one individual and moves backward in time to that individual's ancestors; the opposite of the other two reports. This format is used less frequently because it records two family lines in the same report.

NOTE

The Ahnentafel style assigns the first individual the number 1. His or her father is number 2 and his or her mother is number 3. Men are always even numbers and women are always odd numbers (The exception being when a man is the first individual).

Formatting a Report

You can format other areas of the report as well.

Changing Title and Page Numbering

You can change Family Tree Maker's default settings for title and page number.

1. Click on the **Contents** menu. The Contents menu will appear.

2. Click on **Title & Footnote**. The Title & Footnote for Genealogy Report dialog box will open.

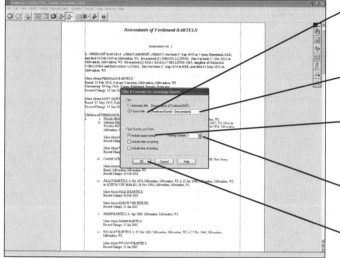

3. Click on the **Custom title** radio button. The cursor will move to the blank field.

4. Type the title you would like displayed in the report.

5. Click in each box in the **Page Number and Date** section, if you want that item to be recorded on the report.

6. Click the up and down arrows to change the **starting number**.

7. Click on **OK**. The Title & Footnote for Genealogy Report dialog box will close.

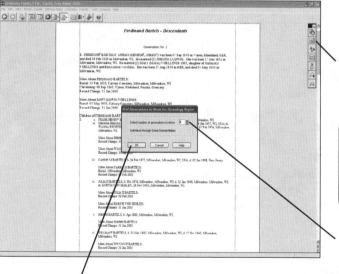

Changing the Number of Generations

1. Click on the **Number of Generations** button in the vertical toolbar.

NOTE

You can also select **# of Generations to Show** from the **Contents** menu. The # of Generations to Show dialog box will open.

2. Click the up and down arrows in the **Select number of generations to show** field to adjust the number.

3. Click on **OK**. The # of Generations to Show for Genealogy Report dialog box will close and the number of generations you have chosen will show on the chart.

Including Notes and Other Options

You can select additional notes you recorded in other areas of the Family File to include in your printed reports. You can also include source information (see Creating Endnotes below). In order to make these selections, make sure your genealogy report is still open.

1. Click on the **Options** button in the side toolbar.

> **NOTE**
>
> You can also click **Options** from the **Contents** menu. The Options for Genealogy Report dialog box will open.

2. Click on the notes check boxes and the radio buttons for sources and generation numbering according to your preferences.

3. Click on **OK**. The Options for Genealogy Report dialog box will close.

> **TIP**
>
> Family Tree Maker turns some of the options on by default. You may want to check your report to verify if you want those default options to show.

Creating Endnotes

You can print source information at the end of a report as endnotes. Before following these steps, make sure your genealogy report is still open.

1. Click on the **Options** button in the side toolbar.

2. Click on the **Include source information as endnotes** radio button. The option will be selected.

3. Click on **OK**. The Options for Genealogy Report dialog box will close.

4. Click the scroll bar to go to the bottom of the report to view the source information.

Creating a Bibliography

The bibliography report lists all the sources you used in your research.

1. Click on the **Reports** button in the main toolbar. A drop-down menu will open.

2. Click **Bibliography**. The Bibliography report will be generated.

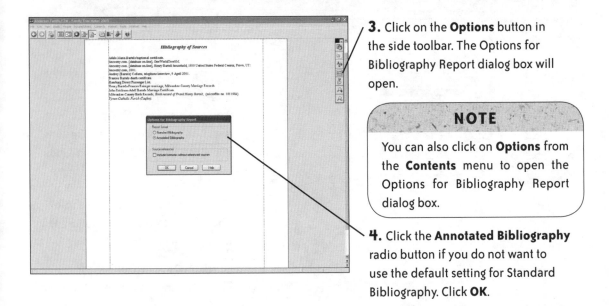

3. Click on the **Options** button in the side toolbar. The Options for Bibliography Report dialog box will open.

> **NOTE**
>
> You can also click on **Options** from the **Contents** menu to open the Options for Bibliography Report dialog box.

4. Click the **Annotated Bibliography** radio button if you do not want to use the default setting for Standard Bibliography. Click **OK**.

> **NOTE**
>
> The annotated bibliography includes the full source citation and comments by the researcher about the source.

Creating a Report of Facts with Sources (Documented Events Report)

The Documented Events Report lists all of the events for which you have source information. Conversely, you can choose to show all of the events for which you do not have source information.

1. Click **Documented Events** from the **Report** button in the main toolbar. The Documented Events report will open.

NOTE

If you already have a custom report open, you can click on **Document Events** from the **Format** button in the vertical toolbar.

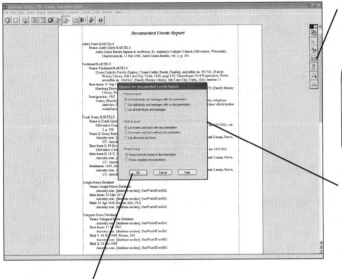

2. Click on the **Options** button in the side toolbar.

NOTE

You can also select **Options** from the **Contents** menu. The Options for Documented Events Report dialog box will open.

3. Click the radio buttons to select which type of individuals to display (those with sources or those without sources or all), what information to display (events with or without sources or all), and how to display the source information.

4. Click **OK**. The Options for Documented Events Report dialog box will close.

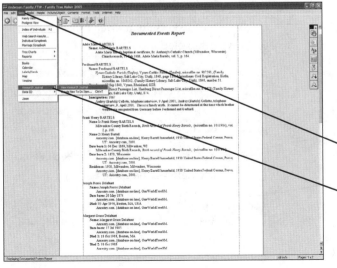

Creating a Research Journal

The Research Journal allows you to track your research and make notes on to-do items within Family Tree Maker.

1. Select **Research Journal** from the **View** menu. A fly-out menu will appear.

2. Click **View Research Journal** from the fly-out menu. The My Research Journal page will appear.

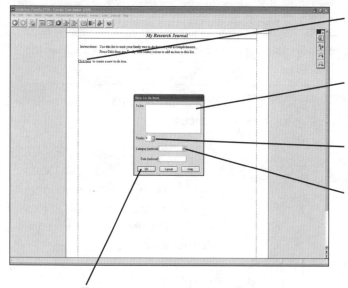

3. Click on the **Click here** hyperlink. The New To-Do Item dialog box will open.

4. Enter your to-do item in the **To-Do** field, e.g., "Look for Aunt Marge in 1930 census."

5. Click on the arrows in the **Priority** field to select a priority for the task.

6. If desired, type a category in the **Category** field. Suggested category topics can be the type of research (e.g., Census or Church Records) or family group (e.g., Smiths, Jones, or Lees).

7. Click on **OK**. The New To-Do Item dialog box will close.

Viewing Done or Not Done Items

The Research Journal is your road map of the research you have done and the research that still must be accomplished. There will be times when you will want to see it all, and other times when you will want to see only what you have done or what is left to do. To use

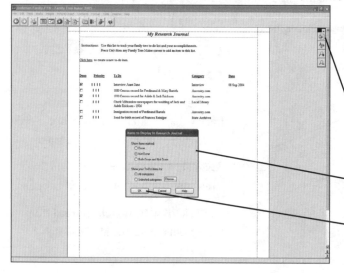

the done check boxes to keep track of your tasks, click inside the **Done** boxes next to each item when a task has been completed.

1. Click on the **Items to Display** button in the vertical toolbar. The Items to Display in Research Journal dialog box will open.

2. Click a **Show items marked** option. The item will be selected.

3. Click on **OK**. The Items to Display in Research Journal dialog box will close.

NOTE

The Research Journal will reflect the changes in the items listed based on whether the To-Do item has been done or is still pending.

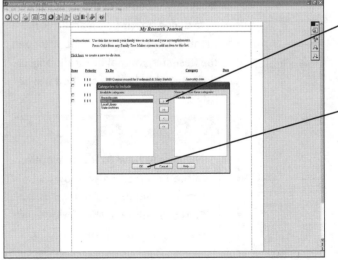

Viewing Items for a Certain To-Do Category

Another way to affect the format of the Research Journal is through the To-Do categories. Usually based on resources or repositories, the To-Do categories allow you to narrow the focus of the report to just those entries for the selected category or categories.

1. Click on the **Items to Display** button in the vertical toolbar. The Items to Display in Research Journal dialog box will open.

2. Click on the **Choose button** in the **Show your To-Do items for** box. The Categories to Include dialog box will open. This dialog box resembles and functions the same as the Individuals to Include dialog box.

3. Click on items you want to include in the left column, and move them to the right column by clicking the **right angle bracket** button. Click **OK** to save the list.

4. Click on **OK** in the two dialog boxes. The Categories to Include dialog box will close, then the Items to Display in Research Journal dialog box will close, and the Research Journal will reflect your changes.

TIP

If you want to delete a To-Do item that you have created, click on the item so that it is highlighted and then press the **Delete** key.

Adding a To-Do Item Anytime

While the Research Journal report is useful, you do not have to go to the Research Journal to add a new to-do item. You can add a new to-do item any time you want. This feature is most useful when adding new research.

1. Click the **Family View** button. The Family View will appear.

2. Click **Research Journal** from the **View** menu.

3. Click on **Create New To Do Item** from the Research Journal fly-out menu. The New To Do Item dialog box will open.

4. Type your entry in the New To Do Item dialog box as you learned earlier in this chapter. The next time you open the Research Journal the additional to-do items added in this method will be listed.

TIP

The **Create New To Do Item** option in the **Edit** menu also shows a hot key combination. You can press **Ctrl+t** to open the New To Do Item dialog box and skip steps 1-3.

10

Creating Specialty and Custom Reports

In addition to its many trees and genealogy reports, Family Tree Maker also includes a number of other reports that allow you to understand the information you have in your database and how the individuals might be related. In this chapter, you'll learn how to:

- View and format Family Group Sheets
- View and format Outline Descendant and Kinship reports
- View and format Alternate Facts reports
- View and format Address, Medical Information, and Living Individual reports
- View and format Marriage and Parentage reports
- View and format Data Errors reports
- View and format Timelines, Maps, Calendars, Labels, and Cards
- View and format Custom Reports

Family Tree Maker offers a variety of specialty reports, such as kinship reports, data errors, timelines, maps, address reports, birthday lists, mailing labels, and calendars. You can also create your own custom report. In this chapter, we'll cover the different types of specialty reports and what you can do to customize these reports, as well as how to generate your own custom report.

Viewing and Formatting Specialty Reports

The specialty reports available in Family Tree Maker include text reports that are likely to be of interest to you as well as more graphical reports such as maps, timelines, and calendars. All of the textual reports can be accessed through the Reports button on the toolbar or the View menu. The more graphical reports are available through the View menu. This section explains each type of report and what changes can be made to the Contents and Format of each report, as the options differ by report.

To open a report:

1. Click on the **Reports** button on the toolbar.

2. Click on the report you would like see. The report will open.

These same steps are used to open and view all of the reports covered in this chapter.

Family Group Sheet

A family group sheet is one of the most commonly used reports in genealogy. It is a detailed report about a single family (primarily the parents and children of a family although it also includes the names of the main couple's parents), including names, birth information, death information, marriage information, notes, and sources. You can also add images for each individual in Family Tree Maker's family group sheet. Family Tree Maker allows you to make many customizations to the family group sheet, including what information to include, how the page is laid out, titles and footnotes, and how the text appears in size, color, and shape.

Items to Include and Options

You can customize the items you include in your group sheets.

1. Click **Items to Include in Family Group Sheet** from the **Contents** menu. The Items to Include in Family Group Sheet dialog box will open.

2. You can add any of the items in the Available items column into the **Your Family Group Sheet contains** column if you want to include them on your family group sheet.

Simply click on the item you want to include in the left column, then press the right angle bracket to move the item to the right column. If **Standard Page** is not in your **Your Family Group Sheet contains** column, select it from the Available Items list on the left, then press the right angle bracket to move the selection to the **Your Family Group Sheet contains** column.

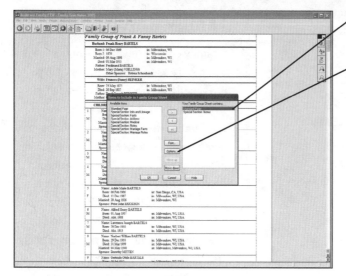

3. Click **Standard Page** in the **Your Family Group Sheet contains** column.

4. Click the **Options** button. (The Options button is grayed out until you click on an item in the right-hand column.) The Options: Standard Page dialog box will open.

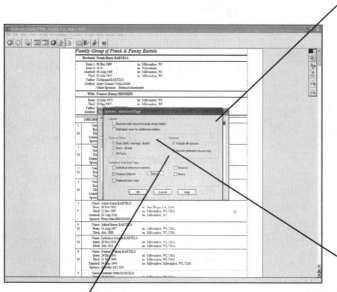

5. Click in the **Layout** check boxes if you want to add headings for which you have not yet entered information (e.g., a blank Died row), and blank rows for children that have not yet been added.

TIP

Click the check boxes for Layout if you want to print the group sheet to take with you on a research trip or to send to family members, to have them fill in the blanks they know.

---

6. Click in the **Facts to Show** radio buttons to specify which details you want to appear in the family group sheet.

7. Click in the **Spouses** radio buttons to specify if you want all spouses to appear in your group sheet, or just the preferred spouse.

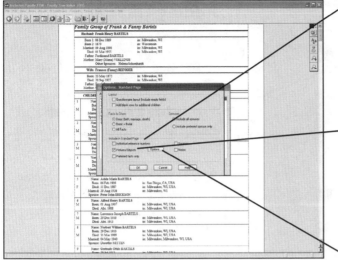

8. Click in the **Include in Standard Page** check boxes to indicate which of the listed items you would like to appear in your group sheet. The Pictures/Objects check box has additional options.

9. Click to add a check mark if the Pictures/Objects checkbox is blank. If you have added images to your scrapbook (see Chapter 7), they will appear in your family group sheet when you close this dialog box.

10. Click the **Options** button. The Options: Pictures/Objects on Family Group Sheet dialog box will open.

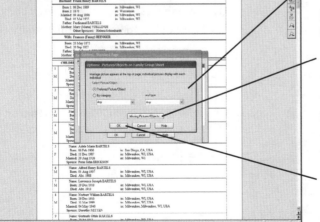

11. Click the radio button to indicate if you want to display images that are preferred, or that fall within a certain category or type.

12. Click the **Missing Pictures/Objects** button. The Missing Pictures/Objects dialog box will open. Select an image you want to show if no image is available – either **None**, a flourish, or a custom picture.

13. Click **OK** to close each dialog box and save your changes.

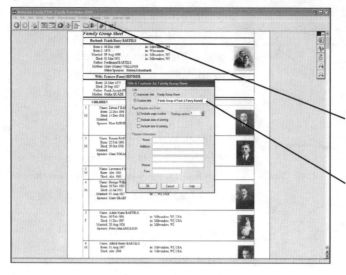

Adding Titles and Footnotes

You can add titles and footnotes to your family group sheets.

1. Click **Title & Footnote** from the **Contents** menu. The Title & Footnote dialog box will appear.

2. Click the **Custom title** radio button to change the default title (Family Group Sheet), and type the new title in the adjoining field.

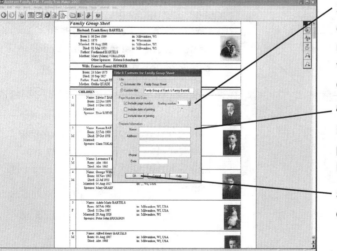

3. Click the **Page Number and Date** check boxes if you want to add a page number (also, select which number you would like to be the starting number), date, and/or time.

4. Enter your contact information in each field that you want to be part of the footnote in the **Preparer Information** box.

5. Click **OK** to save your changes and close the dialog box.

Separate Page Family Group Sheets

If you choose to include additional information for each person (e.g., notes, medical information, etc.) you can have that information appear on separate pages for each individual.

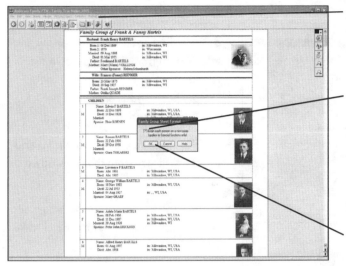

1. Click **Family Group Sheet Format** from the **Format** menu. The Family Group Sheet Format dialog box will appear.

2. Click in the check box if you want each person in your group sheet to appear on a separate page. This applies to any Special Sections you have added to your group sheet from the Customize Your Group Sheet instructions in the previous section.

3. Click **OK** to close the dialog box and save your changes.

Text Font, Style, & Size for Family Group Sheet

You can determine how to format particular items in your group sheet according to font, size, style, and color.

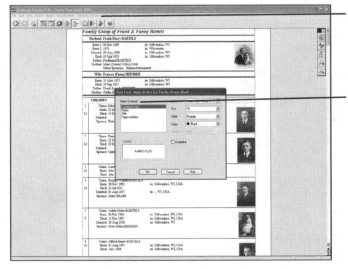

1. Click **Text Font, Style, & Size** from the **Format** menu, select. The Text Font, Style, & Size for Family Group Sheet dialog box will appear.

2. Click on an item you would like to format. In the **Items to format** box, select the items for which you would like to apply a new style. You can click on and format one item at a time, or hold down the Ctrl button and click on several items to format several items at once. The item(s) will be highlighted to indicate they have been selected.

> **TIP**
>
> Changes you make will appear in the Sample box. You c an select and change more than
> one item's attributes at the same time by pressing and holding the control key and click-
> ing on the items, e.g. Title, Footnote.

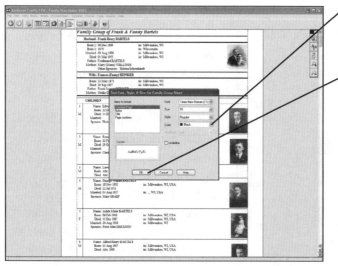

3. Click the **Font** drop-down arrow and select a font from the drop-down list. The font you select will appear in the Sample box so you can view it before accepting your changes.

4. Click the **Size** drop-down arrow and select a font size from the drop-down list.

5. Click the **Style** drop-down arrow and select a font style from the drop-down list.

6. Click the **Color** drop-down arrow and select a font color from the drop-down list.

7. Click **OK** to save your changes and close the dialog box.

Outline Descendant Report

This report starts with an ancestor and outlines each generation of descendants. In Outline Descendant Report, you can change the formatting of the report, select which items and individuals to include in the report, select the number of generations to show in a report, select titles and footnotes, select relationship options, and even select border styles.

Outline Descendant Report Format

You can change the way the Outline Descendant Report is formatted.

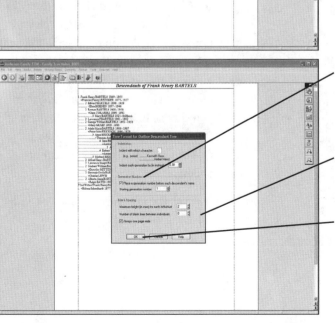

1. Click **Tree Format** from the **Format** menu. The Tree Format for Outline Descendant Tree dialog box will open.

2. Click which character to use for indentions, and how much space you want between each indention, in the **Indention** box. By default, Family Tree Maker indents with an ellipses. You can change the character. For example, if you select "-," Family Tree Maker will use "----"instead of the default, "….."

3. Click the check mark box in the **Generation Numbers** box, if you want to include a generation number before each descendant's name.

4. Click the height of the individual and the number of blank lines between individuals in the **Size & Spacing** box.

5. Click **OK** to close the Tree Format for Outline Descendant Tree dialog box and save your changes.

Items to Include in Outline Descendant Tree

You can select which items to include in Outline Descendant Tree.

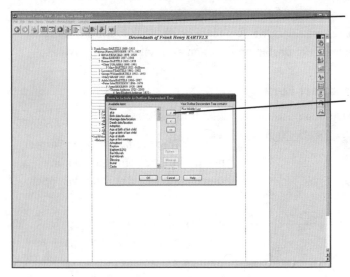

1. Click **Items to Include in each entry** from the **Contents** menu. The Items to Include in Outline Descendant Tree dialog box will open.

2. Select which items to include, following the same steps as the Items to Include dialog box in Family Group Sheets. (Click on an item in the **Available Lists** column, then press the right angle bracket to move the item to the **Your Outline Descendant Tree contains** column.)

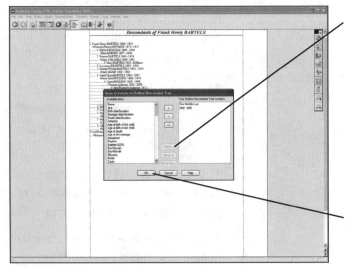

3. When you move an item to the right column, an options dialog may open. If not, you can click on the item in the right column, then press the **Options** button. This will give you the opportunity to make specific selections on each item you choose to include in the Outline Descendant tree, just as you used the Options dialog box in Family Group Sheets.

4. Click **OK** to save your changes and close the dialog box.

Individuals to Include in Outline Descendant Tree

You can select whether to include all descendants or only direct descendants in Outline Descendant Tree.

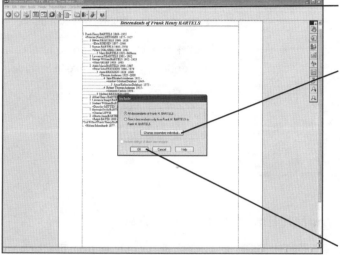

1. Click **Individuals to Include** from the **Contents** menu. The Include dialog box will open.

2. Click which individuals you want to include in your Outline Descendant Tree. If you want to only include the direct descendants from the primary person to a specific descendant, click the **Change Secondary Individual** button to change the selection. (To change the primary individual, go to that individual's Outline Descendant Tree.)

3. Click **OK** to close the dialog box and save your changes.

Number of Generations in Outline Descendant Tree

You can change the number of generations displayed in Outline Descendant Tree.

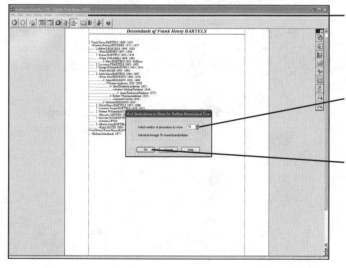

1. Click **# of Generations to Show** from the **Contents** menu. The # of Generations to Show for Outline Descendant Tree dialog box will open.

2. Click the up and down arrow to choose how many generations you would like to show.

3. Click **OK** to save your changes and close the dialog box.

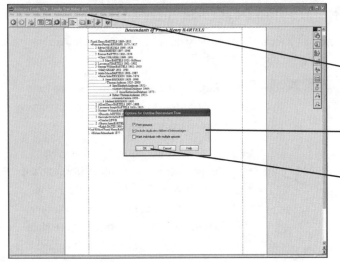

Options for Outline Descendant Tree

1. Click **Options** from the **Contents** menu. The Options for Outline Descendant Tree dialog box will open.

2. Click in each check mark to select what options you would like to include.

3. Click **OK** to save your changes and close the dialog box.

Selecting Borders for your Outline Descendant Tree

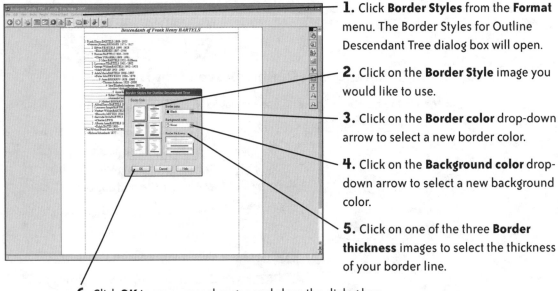

1. Click **Border Styles** from the **Format** menu. The Border Styles for Outline Descendant Tree dialog box will open.

2. Click on the **Border Style** image you would like to use.

3. Click on the **Border color** drop-down arrow to select a new border color.

4. Click on the **Background color** drop-down arrow to select a new background color.

5. Click on one of the three **Border thickness** images to select the thickness of your border line.

6. Click **OK** to save your changes and close the dialog box.

Adding Titles and Footnotes

You can add Titles and Footnotes for Outline Descendant Trees in the same manner as Family Group Sheets, by selecting **Title & Footnote** from the **Contents** menu and making the changes in the dialog box that appears.

Text Font, Style, & Size for Outline Descendant Tree

You can make Text Font, Style, & Size changes to Outline Descendant Trees in the same manner as Family Group Sheets, by selecting **Text Font, Style, & Size** from the **Format** menu and making the changes in the dialog box that appears.

Kinship Report

The Kinship report helps you determine how individuals in your database are related to a specific person. When you select a Kinship Report from the Report button, you will be taken to the Kinship Report of the individual you last viewed.

> **TIP**
>
> Don't forget, you can click on the Index of Individuals button on the toolbar or press F2 to bring up the Index of Individuals and select a new name to be the focus of the report.

In the Kinship report, you can perform several of the same functions you learned about in Outline Descendant Tree. You can add a **Title & Footnote** (under the **Contents** menu), change the **# of Generations to show** (under the **Contents** menu), select a **Border Style** (under the **Format** menu), and select a **Text Font, Style, & Size for Kinship** (under the **Format** menu).

> **NOTE**
>
> While most of these reports have a few functions in common, the dialog box from one report to another may have slightly different functions to accommodate the specific report.

Alternate Facts Report

With the Alternate Facts report, you can view all conflicting facts in your Family File at once. You can double-click on a conflicting fact in the list to open the Edit Individual dialog box and begin making changes if you know the answers for the conflicts.

The Alternate Facts report has several of the options found in Outline Descendant report. You can select which **Individuals to Include** (under the **Contents** menu), add a **Title & Footnote** (under the **Contents** menu), select a **Border Style** (under the **Format** menu), and select a **Text Font, Style, & Size** (under the **Format** menu). In addition, you can sort the Alternate Facts report.

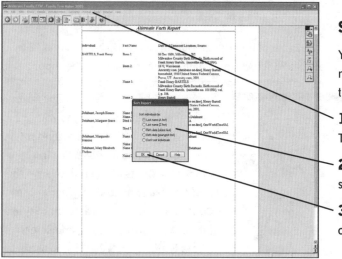

Sort Report

You can change the order in which names and dates are sorted in many of the reports. While in the report:

1. Click on **Sort** from the **Format** menu. The Sort dialog box will open.

2. Click in the radio button next to the sort method you would like to use.

3. Click **OK** to save your changes and close the Sort Report dialog box.

Address Report

The Address report may be useful for correspondence to living relatives or to keep track of an ancestor's main residence. When you select the Address report from the Reports button, it will list all names, addresses, and phone numbers you have entered in your Family File.

The Address report allows you to use several functions already covered in this chapter: select which **Individuals to Include** (under the **Contents** menu), add a **Title & Footnote** (under the **Contents** menu), **Sort your report** (under the **Format** menu), select a **Border Style** (under the **Format** menu) and select a **Text Font, Style, & Size** (under the **Format** menu). In addition, you can select the **Maximum Width for Each Column**.

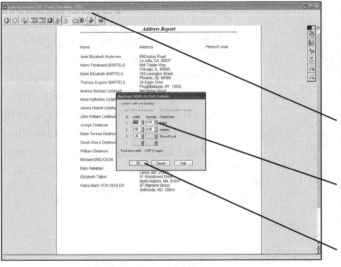

Adjusting Column Widths

You may want to increase the width of your columns to fit longer names. To select the maximum width for each column:

1. Click **Maximum Width** from the **Format** menu. The Maximum Width for Each Column dialog box will open.

2. Click the up and down arrows, or simply type in the fields, to select the width and spacing for each column item.

3. Click **OK** to save your changes and close the Maximum Width for Each Column dialog box.

Medical Information Report

The Medical Information report lists the name, birth date, cause of death, and any other medical information you have entered about individuals in the Medical tab of the Edit Individual dialog box for each individual. This is especially useful for seeing trends in your family's health history.

The Medical Information report allows you to use several functions already covered in this chapter: select which **Individuals to Include** (under the **Contents** menu), add a **Title & Footnote** (under the **Contents** menu), select the **Maximum Width for Each Column** (under the **Format** menu), **Sort your Report** (under the **Format** menu), select a **Border Style** (under the **Format** menu) and select a **Text Font, Style, & Size** (under the **Format** menu).

Birthdays of Living Individuals Report

Family Tree Maker gathers all known birthdays of living individuals into the Birthday report. If the individual does not have a death date recorded and would still be under 120 years old, the program assumes the individual is still living.

The Birthdays of Living Individuals report allows you to use several functions already covered in this chapter: select which **Individuals to Include** (under the **Contents** menu), add a **Title & Footnote** (under the **Contents** menu), select the **Maximum Width for Each Column** (under the **Format** menu), **Sort your Report** (under the **Format** menu), select a **Border Style** (under the **Format** menu) and select a **Text Font, Style, & Size** (under the **Format** menu).

Marriage Report

The Marriage report lists the names of the husbands, wives, the marriage date, and the relationship status for all marriages entered in Family Tree Maker.

The Marriage report allows you to use several functions already covered in this chapter: add a **Title & Footnote** (under the **Contents** menu), select the **Maximum Width for Each Column** (under the **Format** menu), **Sort your Report** (under the **Format** menu), select a **Border Style** (under the **Format** menu) and select a **Text Font, Style, & Size** (under the **Format** menu).

Parentage Report

The Parentage report lists each individual, the individual's parents, and the relationship between the individual and parents (e.g., natural, adopted, foster).

The Parentage report allows you to use several functions already covered in this chapter: select which **Individuals to Include** (under the **Contents** menu), add a **Title & Footnote** (under the **Contents** menu), select the **Maximum Width for Each Column** (under the **Format** menu), **Sort your Report** (under the **Format** menu), select a **Border Style** (under the **Format** menu) and select a **Text Font, Style, & Size** (under the **Format** menu).

Data Errors

The Data Errors report lists all instances where there is missing data or where Family Tree Maker believes there may be a mistake. This includes nonsensical dates (e.g., an individual being born before their parents were born), empty fields, duplicate individuals, name typos and more.

The Data Errors report allows you to use several functions already covered in this chapter: select which **Individuals to Include** (under the **Contents** menu), add a **Title & Footnote** (under the **Contents** menu), select **Options** (under the **Contents** menu), **Sort your Report** (under the **Format** menu), select a **Border Style** (under the **Format** menu) and select a **Text Font, Style, & Size** (under the **Format** menu).

*Family Tree Maker offers a few more specialized reports that are more graphical in nature, and can be found under the **View** menu.*

Timeline

To open the Timeline, click **Timeline** from the **View** menu. The Timeline displays a horizontal bar for each individual depicting his/her lifespan in a chronological chart. The Timeline also includes many significant historical events. You can choose to display these historical milestones to put the lives of your ancestors in historical context.

Timeline Format

To make special customizations to your Timeline Format:

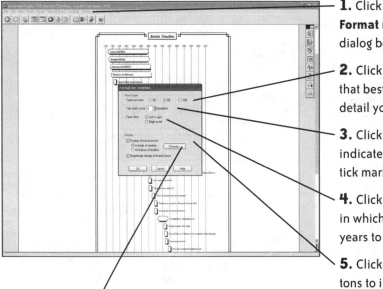

1. Click **Timeline Format** from the **Format** menu. The Format for Timeline dialog box will open.

2. Click the **Years per inch** radio button that best suits you to show how much detail you want squeezed into an area.

3. Click the up and down arrows to indicate where you would like to show tick marks.

4. Click the radio button to indicate in which direction you would like the years to show.

5. Click the check boxes and radio buttons to indicate if you want to display historical events in the **Display** box, and how you would like to display them.

6. Click the **Choose** button to open the Choose Historical Events dialog box.

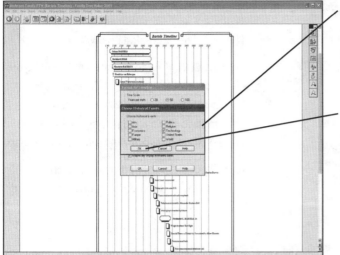

7. Click the check boxes to indicate which historical events you would like to display, ranging from arts to religion. You can choose as many historical events as you desire.

8. Click the **OK** button to save your change and close the dialog box, then click **OK** to close the previous dialog box.

The Timeline also allows you to use several functions already covered in this chapter: select which **Individuals to Include** and **Items to Include** (under the **Contents** menu), add a **Title & Footnote** (under the **Contents** menu), **Sort your Report** (under the **Format** menu), select a **Box, Line and Border Style** (under the **Format** menu) and select a **Text Font, Style, & Size** (under the **Format** menu).

TIP

You can also add the Timeline button to the toolbar if you use it often. You can customize your toolbar in the Preferences dialog box found under the **File** menu, which will be covered in Chapter 16.

Maps

To open the Map, click **Map** from the **View** menu. Family Tree Maker displays a U.S. map with labeled dots marking cities where events you have entered in your Family File took place, e.g., dates and locations where ancestors were born. You can change the appearance of the map by changing the Map Format and Size.

Changing the Map Format

1. Click **Map Format** from the **Format** menu. The Map Format dialog box will open.

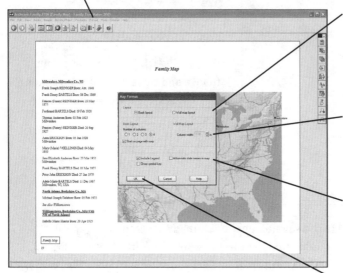

2. Click the radio button with the layout you prefer in the Map Format dialog box. The Book layout will format the map to fit on a single page, while the Wall map layout will create a larger map.

3. Click in the radio buttons, check boxes, or up and down arrows, depending on which layout you choose, the Book Layout or Wall Map Layout.

4. Click the check mark boxes if you want to add a Legend, symbol key, or if you want to abbreviate state names in a map.

5. Click **OK** to save your changes and close the dialog box.

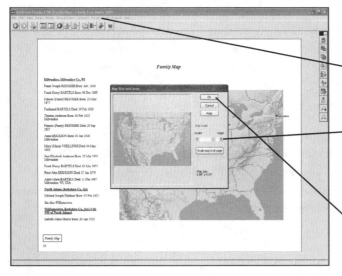

Changing the Map Size and Area

1. Click **Map Size and Area** from the **Format** menu. The Map Size and Area dialog box will open.

2. Drag the scroll block on the Map Scale indicator to make the map larger or smaller, or click the **Scale map to fit page** button.

3. Click **OK** to close the dialog box and save your changes.

You can also change the map to cover another areas besides the United States. Click **Change Map** from the **Format** menu, then select the map you want to use from the Change Map dialog box.

The Map also allows you to use several functions already covered in this chapter: select which **Individuals to Include** and **Items to Include** (under the **Contents** menu), add a **Title & Footnote** (under the **Contents** menu), select **Options** (under the **Contents** menu), and select a **Text Font, Style, & Size** (under the **Format** menu).

> **TIP**
>
> You can add the Maps button to the toolbar if you use it often by customizing the toolbar through the Preferences dialog box found under the File menu.

Calendar

To open the Calendar, click **Calendar** from the **View** menu. The calendar displays all birthdays or anniversaries added to your Family File, or both. Use the scroll bar to move the page down and see each month. You can make some significant changes to your calendar's appearance by selecting which items to include and what basic style you want to give your calendar.

Items to include in Your Calendar

You can select which items to include in your calendar.

1. Click **Items to Include in Calendar** from the **Contents** menu. The Items to include in Calendar dialog box will open.

2. Click the drop-down arrows to select the calendar year and month you want to cover.

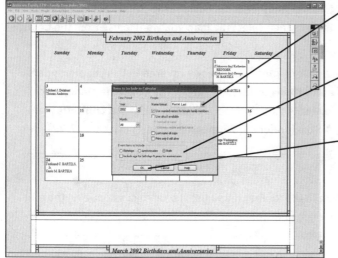

3. Click the **Name format** drop-down arrow to select the way you would like names to appear in the calendar.

4. Click the check boxes that indicate what items you want to include in your calendar.

5. Click **OK** to close the Items to Include in Calendar dialog box.

Box, Line, & Border Styles for Calendar

You can select which Box, Line, & Border Styles to include in your calendar.

1. Click Box, Line, & Border Styles for Calendar from the **Format** menu. The Box, Line, & Border Styles for Calendar dialog box will open.

2. Click the **Box & Line Style** button you would prefer to use.

3. Click the drop-down arrow to select the **Line color** you would like to use.

4. Click the drop-down arrow to select the **Fill color** you would like to use.

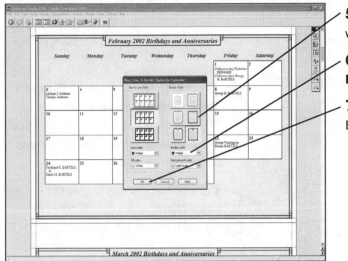

5. Click the **Border Style** button you would prefer to use.

6. Click the drop-down arrow to select **Border color** and **Background color**.

7. Click **OK** to close the Box, Line, & Border Styles dialog box.

The calendar also allows you to use several other functions covered in this chapter: select which **Individuals to Include**, add a **Title & Footnote** (under the **Contents** menu), and select a **Text Font, Style, & Size** (under the **Format** menu).

> **TIP**
>
> You can also add the Calendar button to the toolbar if you use it often by customizing the toolbar through the Preferences dialog box found under the **File** menu.

Mailing Labels and Cards

To open the Labels and Cards template, click **Labels and Cards** from the **View** menu. Family Tree Maker can print labels or cards in a variety of sizes and shapes, depending on the type of label. By default, the labels or cards include some basic information about your family. You can change this information.

The Mailing Labels and Cards feature includes the following functions covered in other areas of this chapter: **Items to Include**, **Individuals to Include**, **Options** (all under the **Contents** menu), **Maximum Width for Each Picture/Object**, **Sort Labels/Cards**, and **Text, Font, Style and Size**, and **Box and Line Styles** (all under the **Format** menu).

Print Setup for Labels and Cards

It is important to use the right setup for Labels and Cards because they do not print to standard 8 ½" by 11" paper like most reports.

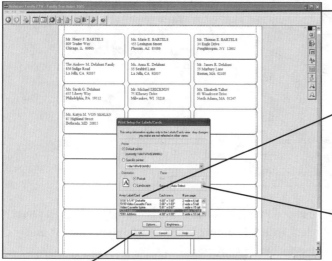

1. Click Print Setup from the **File** menu. The **Print Setup for Labels/Cards** dialog box will open. Mostly likely, you will want to keep the default settings for Default printer and Print Orientation.

2. Click the description in **Avery Label/Card**, which best matches the type of labels or cards you are using. The label number is typically on the box packaging.

3. You may need to click **Manual** from the Source drop-down menu to manually feed your labels into your printer.

4. Click **OK** to save your print setup changes, before going to **Print Labels/Cards** from the **File** menu.

> ### TIP
>
> To sort your labels and cards, select Sort Labels and Cards from the Format menu. Then make your selection in the Sort Labels/Cards dialog box.

Custom Reports

Custom Reports allow you to create reports with your own criteria. For example, just as Family Tree Maker can create a custom report for Birthdays of Living Individuals, you can create a custom report for Favorite Ice Cream if you have recorded that information for several individuals in your Family File. The Custom Report defaults to a list of all individuals, birth dates, and death dates, so you can begin to customize it with all information intact.

To begin, click the **Report** button and then click **Custom**. The Custom report will open.

Choosing Individuals to Include in Your Report

Begin by selecting which individuals you want to include in your report.

1. Click on the **Individuals to Include** button on the vertical toolbar.

2. If you do not want to include all individuals in your file, click the **Individuals to Include** button. The Individuals to Include dialog box will open.

3. Click to select an individual you want to include in the **Available individuals** list.

4. Click on the right angle bracket button to move one individual.

5. Click on the **Ancestors** button to include an individual and all of the individual's ancestors, or the **Descendants** button to include an individual and all of the individual's descendants.

6. Click on **OK**. The Individuals to Include dialog box will close and your changes will be saved.

Adding Items to Include in Your Report

When customizing your report, you can also select which items to include in your report.

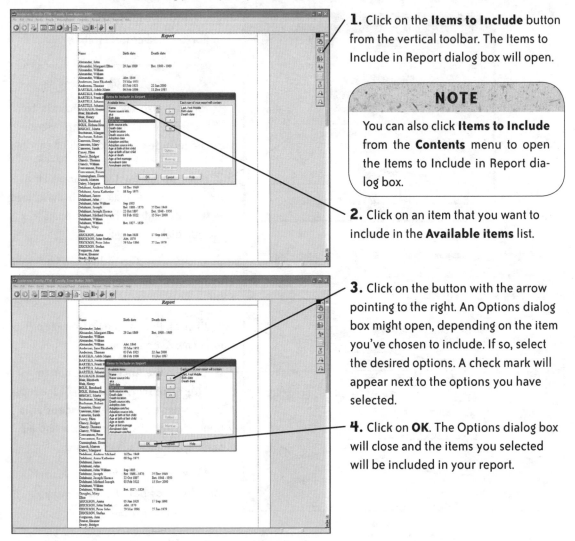

1. Click on the **Items to Include** button from the vertical toolbar. The Items to Include in Report dialog box will open.

> ### NOTE
>
> You can also click **Items to Include** from the **Contents** menu to open the Items to Include in Report dialog box.

2. Click on an item that you want to include in the **Available items** list.

3. Click on the button with the arrow pointing to the right. An Options dialog box might open, depending on the item you've chosen to include. If so, select the desired options. A check mark will appear next to the options you have selected.

4. Click on **OK**. The Options dialog box will close and the items you selected will be included in your report.

Using the Find Button to Define More Specific Criteria

You may want to create a report with more specific criteria. For example, you may want to generate a report showing all individuals who were born in a particular city.

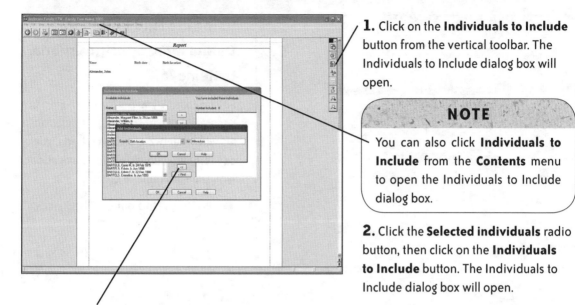

1. Click on the **Individuals to Include** button from the vertical toolbar. The Individuals to Include dialog box will open.

> **NOTE**
>
> You can also click **Individuals to Include** from the **Contents** menu to open the Individuals to Include dialog box.

2. Click the **Selected individuals** radio button, then click on the **Individuals to Include** button. The Individuals to Include dialog box will open.

3. Click the left double angle bracket button (**<<**) to clear individuals from the list on the right. If you do not clear the list, the individuals in the right box will be included whether or not they meet the criteria you are about to set.

Find >

4. Click on the **Find>** button (make sure the arrow is pointing to the right).

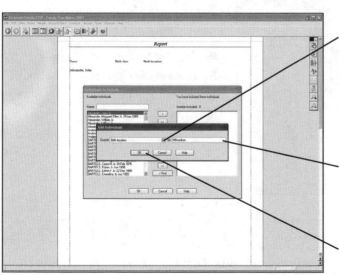

5. Click on the down arrow in the **Search** field. The Search drop-down list will appear.

6. Click to select the field for which you want to set the criteria, such as birth location.

7. Press the **Tab** key. The cursor will move to the **for** field. Type the date, name, etc. you seek, such as the name of a city.

8. Click on **OK**. The list on the right will now include individuals who meet the criteria you have set.

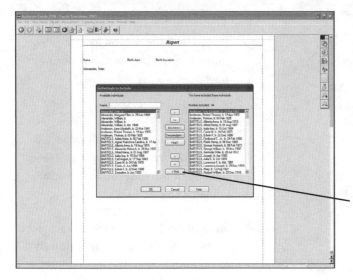

Using the Find Button to Define More Specific Criteria to Remove

Similar to how you performed a Find to generate a report showing all individuals who matched a certain criteria, you can remove individuals you have added with the Find remove button.

1. Click the **<Find** button. The Remove Individuals dialog box will open.

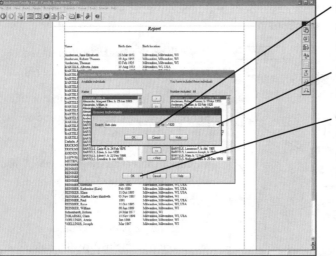

2. Click the **Search** drop-down arrow and select which item you would like to remove.

3. Click in the **for** field and type in the name, date, etc., you want to remove.

4. Click **OK** to save your changes. Relatives in the right column that match that criteria will be moved back to the left column.

TIP

You can use operators such as less than (<) and greater than (>) when you set your criteria. For a full list of options, click on the **Help** button in the Add Individuals or Remove Individuals dialog box.

In addition to specifying individuals and items to include in your custom report, you can also add a **Title & Footnote** (under the **Contents** menu), select the **Maximum Width for Each Column** (under the **Format** menu), **Sort your Report** (under the **Format** menu), select a **Border Style** (under the **Format** menu) and select a **Text Font, Style, & Size** (under the **Format** menu). These features were all covered earlier in the chapter with different reports, and will function in a similar way for custom reports.

Exporting Reports to Other File Formats

You may want to export your reports to other file formats, to share with others or to aid in your research. Make sure your report is open.

1. Click on **File**. The File menu will appear.

2. Click **Export Report**. A fly-out menu will appear.

3. From the fly-out menu, select how you would like to export your report. Your options are:

Acrobat (PDF) – This format retains printer formatting and graphical elements so it resembles how the printed document will appear. You cannot make changes to the PDF from within Family Tree Maker, and you need the free Adobe® Reader® in order to read it. The Reader can be downloaded from the Adobe website.

Plain Text (TXT) – This format does not retain any of the formatting. This is a version that can be typically opened by any word processing or document-editing program and can be edited and resaved.

Word-Processor (RTF) – This format is based on a basic text file, but it can include information such as text style, size, and color. Also, this is a universal format, so it can be read by nearly all word processors.

Spreadsheet (CSV) – This format organizes information into fields (comma-separated values) and is meant to be imported into spreadsheet programs. Only reports in columnar format can be exported to this format.

NOTE

Not all reports can be exported to all formats. For example, reports with graphical elements, such as the Family Group Sheet and the Outline Descendant Tree, can only be exported to PDF format.

Once you have made your selection, the Export Report dialog box will open.

4. Type in a name for the file in the **File name** field.

5. Click **Save** to save the file in the directory shown or open a different directory to save the file to a different location. The file will be saved and the Export Report dialog box will close.

PART IV

Searching With Family Tree Maker

11

Using Family Tree Maker to Help You Research Your Tree

Many of the views, charts, and reports in Family Tree Maker help you to see gaps in your research. Family Tree Maker helps you fill in these gaps by searching Ancestry.com for more information on the people in your Family File. You can also easily add the information Family Tree Maker finds on Ancestry.com through a Web Merge Wizard. In this chapter, you'll learn how to:

- Use the automatic search feature
- Set a search criteria
- View Web Search report
- Understand the Web Search report
- Use the Web Merge wizard

If you are connected to the Internet, Family Tree Maker 2005 will automatically search Ancestry.com for information about individuals in your Family File. You can view the results of this search in a Web Search report, filter your search results, and even merge the results into your Family File.

Understanding the Automatic Search Feature

If you open Family Tree Maker while you do not have an Internet connection, the application will display a No Internet Connectivity dialog box. If you are connected to the Internet, a star will appear in the Web Search buttons in Family View and Pedigree View when Web Search has found a match that meets the search criteria you have chosen. However, even if Web Search results do not meet the criteria you have chosen, you can still click the Web Search buttons to go to the Web Search report. The Web Search button in the toolbar does not change, and you can always click it to go to the Web Search report.

> ### NOTE
>
> Web Search features in Pedigree View are also discussed in Chapter 5, Navigating and Editing in Pedigree View.

1. The **Web Search** button will alert you with a star when Family Tree Maker has found a result that matches the criteria you have set.

2. The **Web Search** button shows the magnifying glass without a star when the results found do not meet the quality threshold you set. You can still view the search results available by clicking on this button.

Setting a Search Criteria

Set your Family File search criteria for Web Search from Family View or Pedigree View.

> **NOTE**
>
> You can also set your default search criteria from the Preferences dialog box, which will be covered in Chapter 17, or from the Web Search report, which will be covered later in this chapter when you learn about filtering Web Search results.

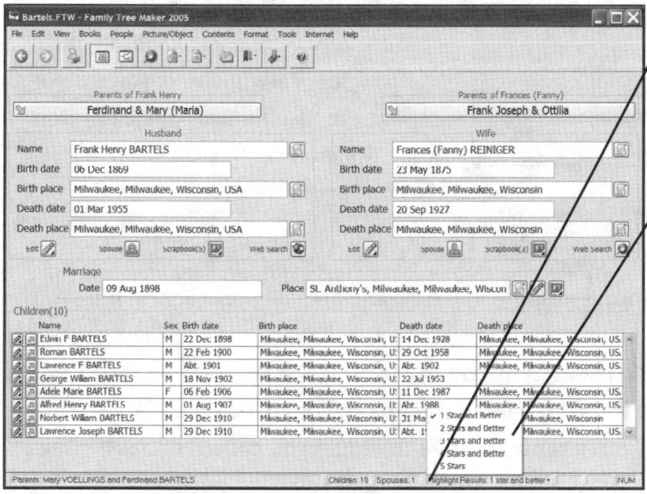

1. Click on the drop-down arrow labeled **Highlight Results** in the status bar at the bottom right section of the screen. A menu will appear.

2. Click the number of stars you would like before Family Tree Maker indicates that search results meeting that quality level exist. A check mark will appear next to the item you chose.

> **NOTE**
>
> The larger the number of stars, the more relevant the search result is likely to be to your ancestor. However, if you restrict your search results too much, you may miss a record that has that elusive information you are missing.

Viewing Web Search Report

You can view the Web Search report at any time, even if Web Search does not match the criteria you set. However, once the Web Search report opens, you may need to change the search criteria in order to see some potential matches. For example, the Web Search report may open and indicate there are no results for a quality level of 5 stars and above, so you may want to change it to 3 stars and above to widen the possibilities.

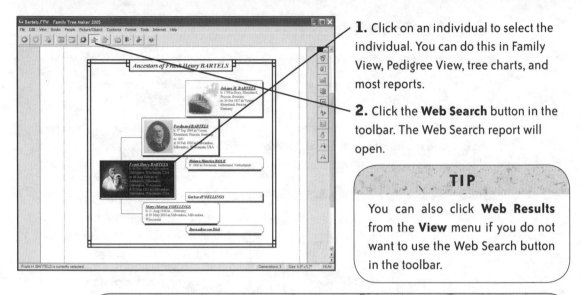

1. Click on an individual to select the individual. You can do this in Family View, Pedigree View, tree charts, and most reports.

2. Click the **Web Search** button in the toolbar. The Web Search report will open.

> ### TIP
>
> You can also click **Web Results** from the **View** menu if you do not want to use the Web Search button in the toolbar.

> ### NOTE
>
> You can view a Web Search report from Family View any time. Simply click on the Web Search button below an individual's name to open that individual's Web Search report. In Pedigree View, click the **Web Search** button in the node if a Web Search result met the criteria you set or click on the **Web Search Results** button in the details area of the Side Panel to view the Web Search report of the individual you clicked on in the tree. The Web Search for … report will open for the individual you have selected.

Understanding the Web Search Report

The Web Search report is divided into three sections.

1. The top half of the report lists the records found on Ancestry.com, with details about each possible match.

2. The bottom left box displays details about the information available in the Ancestry.com record you have highlighted in the top half of the report and is used for Family Tree Maker's Web Merge feature, and to allow you to compare information in your Family File with the Web Search results.

3. The bottom right box displays the details you have entered about the individual in your Family File. This makes it easier for you to compare your information with the potential matches Web Search may have found.

NOTE

To see all of the details available in a record, you must either have a subscription to or be participating in a trial of the associated data collection. You can subscribe or participate in a trial under the Internet menu.

Columns in the top half of the report include:

1. Quality – The number of stars indicates the likelihood of a good match. The more stars listed, the stronger the likelihood of a positive match.

2. Name – The name column lists exactly how the name appears in the source in which it was found.

3. Event – The event column lists the type of event relevant to the source information found, e.g., Birth, Residence, Death.

4. Date – The date listed on the record found.

5. Place – You can often compare the place the record was found with possible locations the ancestor may have been. For example, if the birth record appears in Kentucky, USA, and you know your relative grew up in Kentucky, there is a good possibility this is a good lead.

6. Source – The source in the Ancestry.com collection where the record was discovered by Family Tree Maker. The sources are all hyperlinked so you can click on them to view the exact context for where the record was found if you have a subscription to the source at Ancestry.com. You can also use the Source feature to narrow down your search.

7. Status - The status column lets you make individual notes about each search result: None, Ignore, Follow Up, Merged, or Done.

> **NOTE**
>
> If the name appears in angle brackets < >, the data collection may not have the exact name indexed. This is frequently the case with newspaper or other collections that primarily contain images.

Filter Your Web Search Report Results

You can filter your Web Search report results to view only the results that are most relevant. You can filter by Quality (likelihood of a positive match), Source (where the information was found, e.g., Census Records, Military Records), or Status (e.g., Follow up, Merged)

Sort the Quality Column

1. Click the down arrow above the **Quality** column. A drop-down menu will appear.

2. Click on the number of stars you want a source to have before Family Tree Maker will show the result. A filter will be applied and matches with fewer stars than what you have selected will not appear.

TIP

While the ranking of the stars is an attempt to help you decide which search results to look at first, due to errors by census transcribers etc., you may still find matches in the results with fewer stars. You may want to start with only five-star matches, then move down to four-star matches, and so forth.

NOTE

If you see zero matches, you have narrowed the search too much. For example, you may have indicated you only want to see five-star matches, but if Family Tree Maker has found only four-star matches at best, you will not have any positive search results.

Sort the Source Column

1. Click the **down arrow** above the Source column. A drop-down menu will appear.

2. Click a specific source type if you only want to see results for one source type, or select ALL (the default setting) if you want to see results from all sources. The items in the search results table will change to show only matches found for the source type you have selected. For example, if you only want to see birth, marriage, and death records, select **Birth, Marriage, & Death Records.**

Sort the Status Column

1. Click anywhere in the individual's row. The row will be highlighted and a small down arrow will appear in the Status column.

2. Click on the **down arrow** in the Status column. A drop-down menu will appear.

3. Click **None, Ignore, Follow up, Merged,** or **Done** from the list. Unless you select None, the column will indicate the status you have chosen.

Filter Web Search According to Status Column

1. Click the **down arrow** above the Status column.

2. Click the status by which you want to sort your column:

a. All – Displays all search results: Ignore, Follow Up, Merged, Done, or None.

b. Active – Displays all search results marked as either Follow Up or None.

c. None – Displays all search results that have not been marked.

d. Follow Up – Displays all search results marked Follow Up.

e. Ignore – Displays all search results marked Ignore.

f. Merged – Displays all search results you have merged through the Web Merge Wizard; this status will automatically be set after you merge a result.

g. Done – Displays all search results marked Done.

> **NOTE**
>
> In Web Search results, any status for a result will only apply to that result for that individual, not other individuals in your Family File. In addition, you can always opt to remove the Ignore label.

Using the Web Merge Wizard

If you find results in the Web Search report that you would like to add to your Family File, you can merge them into your file with Family Tree Maker's Web Merge Wizard. You can merge specific individuals and the individual's parents, spouses, and children, as long as those family members are associated with the record Web Search found.

NOTE

Unlike a regular file merge, the Web Merge process will never overwrite any of your data. However, it is always a good idea to save a backup of your file.

Source information will automatically be included for each fact you add to your file, unless you opt to ignore the fact or individual completely. If you do not want source information to be included automatically, you can turn this feature off through Preferences (under the File menu).

To Merge a Result into Your Family File:

1. Click on a Web Search result you would like to merge into your Family File. The information available in the online record will appear in the Selected Person from Web Search box.

2. Click the **Merge** button. The Web Merge Wizard will launch.

3. Click the **Next >** button after you are done reading the welcome text on the Welcome page. The Merge Primary Individual page will open.

NOTE

Click in the check box at the bottom of the Welcome page if you do not want to see the introduction each time you use the Web Merge Wizard.

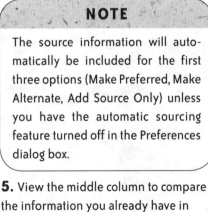

4. Click in the radio buttons of the first column according to what you want to do with the information found on Ancestry.com.

a. Make Preferred – Make the information the preferred fact in your Family File.

b. Make Alternate – Make the information the alternate fact in your Family File.

c. Add Source Only – Only add the source information to the fact in your Family File, e.g., you may already have the same fact listed in your Family File, but you want to add this as another source to further validate your existing fact.

d. Do Nothing – Do not merge the information into your Family File, e.g., you may choose to ignore some facts from the Ancestry.com record, although it is usually a good idea to include all facts from a particular record in case they turn out to be relevant. This option will also ignore source information.

NOTE

The source information will automatically be included for the first three options (Make Preferred, Make Alternate, Add Source Only) unless you have the automatic sourcing feature turned off in the Preferences dialog box.

5. View the middle column to compare the information you already have in your Family File with what you are about to merge into your Family File.

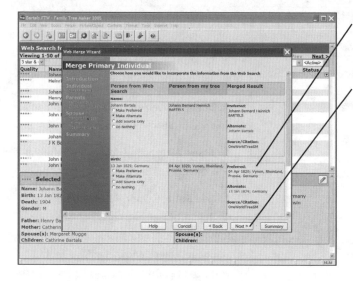

6. View the right-hand column to see how your selections in the first column will affect your Family File.

7. Click **Next >**. If the individual you want to merge has parents, spouse(s), or children that Web Search has found, the Web Merge Wizard will ask you if you want to add the information found for the first additional family member. If the individual does not have siblings or parents associated with this source, click **Next >** to go to the Summary Page and skip to step 10. If the individual does have additional family members, continue to step 8.

NOTE

All names related to a Web Merge are listed in the blue navigation panel on the left side of the Web Merge Wizard. You can click on a name to skip to a specific individual, or let Family Tree Maker methodically go down the list starting at the top.

8. Click the radio button to select if you want to **ignore** the first additional family member, **add** the additional family member as a new individual, or **merge** the additional family member with an existing individual in your Family File. The details about the first additional family member found in Web Search will be in the **Person from Web Search** column, while the information you already have in your Family File will be in the **People from my tree** column, so you can compare the information you have with what Family Tree Maker found. If more than one individual appears in the **People from my tree** column, you will need to select the one with whom you want to merge the new information.

> **NOTE**
>
> If you do not want to go through each name the Web Merge Wizard wants to merge, click **Summary,** then click on the **Merge Now button.** The additional family members will automatically be added if no equivalent family members exist in your file. However, if an immediate family member exists, Family Tree Maker will not default to adding the individuals as new people, since you may want to merge the information into the existing family member(s). In this case, you will default to ignoring the person.

9. Click **Next >**. Follow step 8 with every name in the Wizard until there are no siblings or parents left, and the **Next >** button takes you to the Summary page.

10. Verify your selections in the Summary page. You cannot undo a merge once it has been performed. However, none of your existing information will be overwritten, so if you decide you made a mistake, you can simply delete the fact or source that you added during the merge.

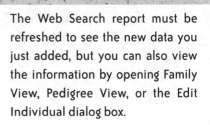

11. Click **Merge Now** in the Summary page. A Family Tree Maker 2005 dialog box will open to tell you when your Web Search result has been successfully merged into your tree.

12. Click **OK** to close the Family Tree Maker 2005 dialog box.

> ### NOTE
>
> The Web Search report must be refreshed to see the new data you just added, but you can also view the information by opening Family View, Pedigree View, or the Edit Individual dialog box.

Searching Data CDs

In addition to a Web Search feature for searching data on Ancestry.com, you can also use Family Tree Maker to view hundreds of data CDs containing information from marriage indexes, passenger and immigration lists, genealogy indexes and more. In this chapter, you'll learn how to:

- Navigate in a data CD

- Read data pages

- Search for names with the Search Expert

- Work with matches

- Exit a data CD

Family Tree Maker can search an extensive data CD-ROM collection sold through Genealogy.com with its built-in CD-ROM viewer. The data CD-ROMs contain information covering records such as: census, birth, marriage and death, military, genealogies, bibliographies, and more.

You can purchase the data CDs individually as they meet your needs, or even obtain the FamilyFinder Index, which is the index of the entire data collection from Genealogy.com. To see what data is available on the more than 300 discs, or to search for which CDs contain possible matches before buying, visit <http://www.genealogy.com/cdhomelist.html >.

The data on these CDs comes in four varieties:

- **Image** – microfilmed images of records, such as census or military records

- **Data** – information from marriage records, death records, and much more

- **Text** – text from books, such as local histories or genealogies

- **World Family Tree** – family trees that were submitted by other family historians

To view a data CD:

1. Click the **View** menu. The View menu will open.

2. Select **Data CD**. A fly-out menu will open.

3. Click **View CD**. The About this Family Archive dialog box will open.

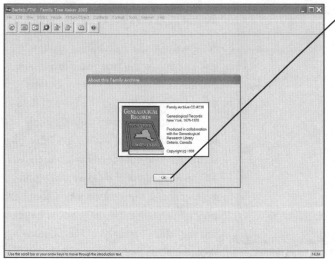

4. Click **OK**. The license agreement dialog box will appear.

5. Read the license agreement, then click **OK**. Family Tree Maker will open to the introduction page of the CD.

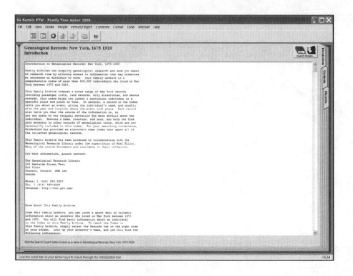

Navigating in a Data CD

Although Family Tree Maker automatically opens to the **Introduction** tab in the data CD, there may be other tabs as well, depending on the type of data CD. For example, many data CDs contain a **Contents** tab, which is a Table of Contents, and a **Records** tab, which lists all the Records in the CD first in alphabetical order, then by locality. Other CDs may contain an **Index** tab, and a **Pages** tab that shows images of the original records.

TIP

You can click and drag the scroll bar to move the text up and down on the page as you read or scan the text, or you can click in the text and use the up and down arrows on your keyboard.

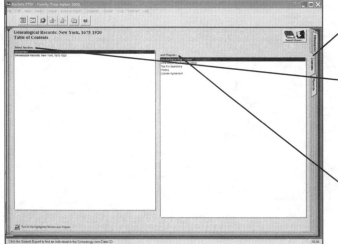

1. Click the **Contents** tab to view the data CD's table of contents.

2. Click on an item in the **Selection Section** to choose an area of the CD which you want to view. The **and Chapter** section will open with a list of each chapter or record section.

3. Double-click on the chapter you want to read. The text or image for that section will open.

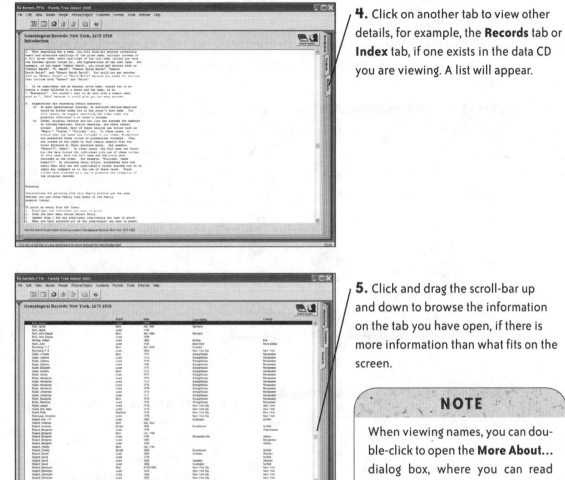

4. Click on another tab to view other details, for example, the **Records** tab or **Index** tab, if one exists in the data CD you are viewing. A list will appear.

5. Click and drag the scroll-bar up and down to browse the information on the tab you have open, if there is more information than what fits on the screen.

NOTE

When viewing names, you can double-click to open the **More About...** dialog box, where you can read additional details about the individual.

NOTE

You can also click the blue Information button for additional information about an individual. The blue button will always appear in the same area of the window if that feature is available for the current data CD.

Reading Pages

Some data CDs, (like those containing family histories), will have pages within, which you can read much like a book. You will know this feature is available if the Pages tab appears when you open the data CD.

Click on the **Pages** tab to view the pages.

Features of the page include:

1. Click and drag the scroll bar to read further down on the page, or vice versa.

2. Click the **Next** button to go to the next page.

3. Click the **Prev** button to go to the previous page.

4. Click the **Magnify** button to increase the size of the text on the page. When you go to a Next or Previous page, Family Tree Maker will revert the new page to the default image size.

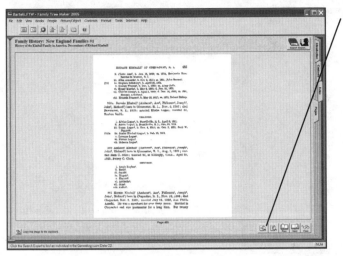

5. Click the **De-magnify** button to decrease the size of the text on the page.

Searching for Names: The Search Expert

The Search Expert is the recommended way to search for a name in CDs, either in the FamilyFinder Index or on the actual data CD. When the Search Expert finds a matching name in the FamilyFinder index, it tells you which data CD contains more information about the name. Reading the information in the data CD will help you determine if you have actually found your ancestor, or just someone with a similar name. When you do find one of your ancestors, you can add information from the data CD directly to the Family File. With many of the data CDs, you can use the Search Expert to select and search on a name from the Family File you have open.

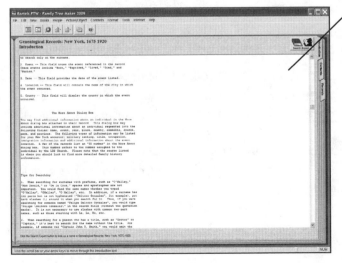

1. Click the **Search Expert**. The Search Expert dialog box will open.

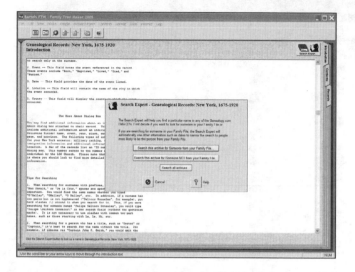

In this example, the Search Expert has three search options, which function in three different ways.

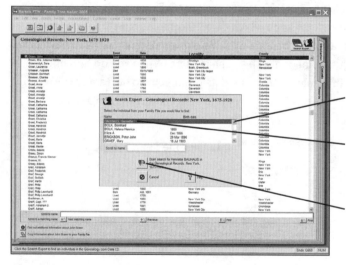

*a. If you click **Search this archive for Someone from your Family File**, a dialog box will open which lists the names of all individuals in your Family File.*

1. Click and drag the scroll bar to move up and down the list of names.

2. Click on a name when you find one that you want Family Tree Maker to search.

3. Click the **Start search for ...** button to have Family Tree Maker search the data CD for that individual. If no match is found, Family Tree Maker will display a dialog box stating that no matches were found. If a match is found, Family Tree Maker will take you back to the Records page with the name highlighted. You can then double-click to view more details about the individual.

NOTE

If your search returns zero results, your ancestor may still be in the record. The individual could be in a record that was not indexed, or the name could have been recorded incorrectly. The FamilyFinder Index is made up of many different sources, including hand-written census records more than a century old, so there can be spelling errors, misinterpretations of names, transpositions of first and last names, first initials being used instead of last names, abbreviated names, and other complications. In addition, if you are searching for a woman in the Social Security Death Index, you will likely need to search under her married name, not her maiden name. You may want to review the introduction tab at the beginning of the CD to search for other hints on finding an individual in that particular data CD.

NOTE

If the data CD contains images, there will be a magnifying glass next to each page number below the image. If the information in the data CD is in records, there will be a magnifying glass to the left of the matches. When a field in a record contains too much information to fit in the allotted space, Family Tree Maker places an ellipsis (…) button to the right. Click the ellipsis button to view the additional information.

*b. If you click **Search this archive for Someone NOT from your Family File**, the Search Expert dialog box will open.*

1. Type information about the individual in the corresponding fields. You may want to include less information for a higher chance of a successful match.

NOTE

On some data CDs, you can search for name only, while in others you can search for other information such as dates and location.

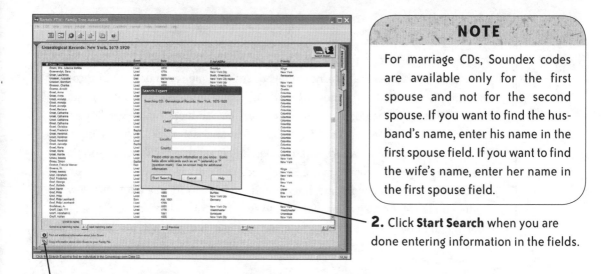

2. Click **Start Search** when you are done entering information in the fields.

*c. If you click **Search all archives ...**, you will need to insert the FamilyFinder Index to search all the FamilyFinder archives for a match. The FamilyFinder Index is a set of CDs containing an index to all of the Family Tree Maker data CDs. This CD set can tell you which CD-ROM(s) contain the records for which you are searching but they do not contain the records themselves.*

Working with Matches

When you find a match, you can further search through it by clicking **Next** to move forward and clicking **Previous** to move backwards through the matches. **First** will take you to the very first match, and **Final** will take you to the last match.

To save a match into your Family File:

1. Click on the name you want to save to your Family File in the Records tab.

2. Click on the **Copy** button. The Copy Information to Family File dialog box will open.

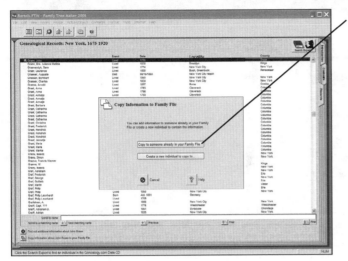

3. Click Copy to someone already in your Family File if you want to add the information found to an existing name in your Family File.

4. Click a name from the list.

5. Click **Copy** information to [name of individual] in your Family File. The Facts to Import dialog box will open.

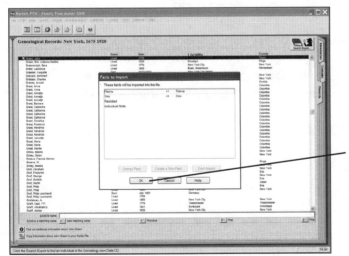

6. View the information in the dialog box to select what information you want to add to the Family File. The list in the left column shows what information will be added to your Family File, and the list in the right column shows what information is already in your Family File.

7. Click **OK** if you are happy with the information you are going to add to your Family File. The Merge Individuals dialog box will open.

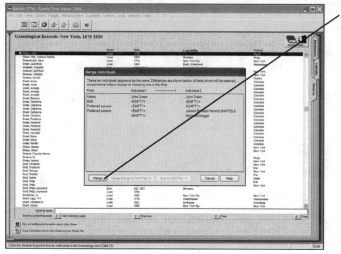

8. Click **Merge**. The information will be merged to your Family File.

Exiting a Data CD

When you are done with your data CD, simply open your CD-ROM drive and take the CD out. Family Tree Maker will not be able to read the CD if the CD is not in the drive. You can insert a new data CD, as long as you are still in **View CD** in Family Tree Maker. Family Tree Maker will automatically view the new data, or, you can click a button in the toolbar to leave the CD data page and go another window, e.g., Family View or Pedigree View.

PART V

Sharing Your Research with Others

13

Creating a Family History Book

For many researchers, the ultimate goal is to publish a record of their ancestry. Family Tree Maker has long offered one of the easiest ways to put a variety of reports together to share with family, friends, or colleagues. Because the process is so easy, you can even create preliminary versions of your book at different stages in the research process. In this chapter, you'll learn how to:

- Select reports and trees to include

- Organize selected items

- Add additional text

- Work with images

- Add page breaks

- Create an index

- Add to a book

- Finalize and share your book

You can create a book complete with charts, reports, photos, stories, and an automatically generated table of contents and index. The book will be saved to a PDF format, allowing others to view or print the book without having to use the Family Tree Maker software program.

Create a New Book

1. Click on **Books** in the menu. The Books menu will open.

2. Click **New Book** from the menu. The New Book dialog box will open.

3. Click in the **Book title** field. Type a title in the Book title field.

4. Click in the **Author** field. Type a name.

5. Click **OK**. The New Book dialog box will close and the Book page will open.

Selecting Specific Reports and Trees to Include

You will create your book by selecting items from the left column and moving them to the right column. The right column represents the outline of your book. You can first create your front matter, such as Foreword, Dedication, Copyright, etc. Then, you'll select Trees and Reports to add to your book.

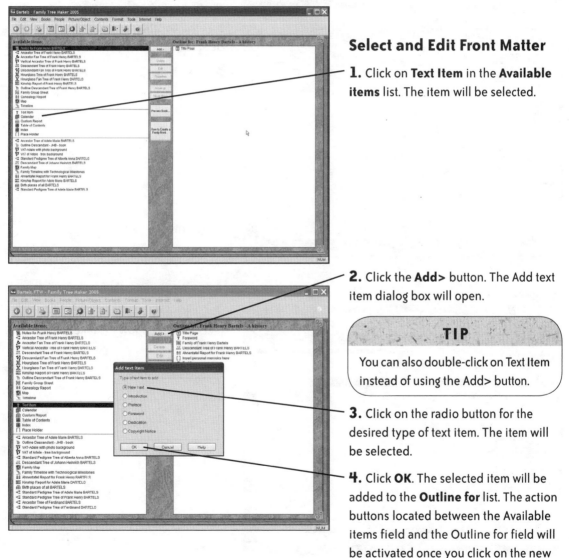

Select and Edit Front Matter

1. Click on **Text Item** in the **Available items** list. The item will be selected.

2. Click the **Add>** button. The Add text item dialog box will open.

TIP

You can also double-click on Text Item instead of using the Add> button.

3. Click on the radio button for the desired type of text item. The item will be selected.

4. Click **OK**. The selected item will be added to the **Outline for** list. The action buttons located between the Available items field and the Outline for field will be activated once you click on the new item you have added to your **Outline for** list.

> **NOTE**
>
> Family Tree Maker automatically adds the Title Page, because this page is required to create the book. It has been placed in the **Outline for** list to indicate it is part of the Book selection.

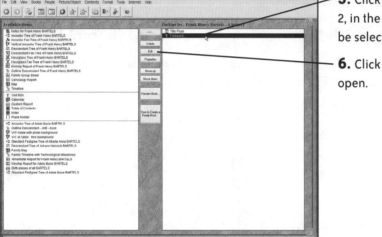

5. Click on the item you selected in step 2, in the **Outline for** field. The item will be selected.

6. Click **Edit**. A text editing window will open.

7. Click on the **toolbar** buttons in the text editing window to make changes to the item.

TIP

The toolbar buttons are similar to those found in word-processing programs. If you click on one of the toolbar buttons, such as italic, before you type, then the text you enter will be in italics. You can also drag your mouse over the word to highlight it, then click a button, like italics, to change the appearance of the word. The most commonly used toolbar buttons are the B for bold, I for Italicize, and U for Underline.

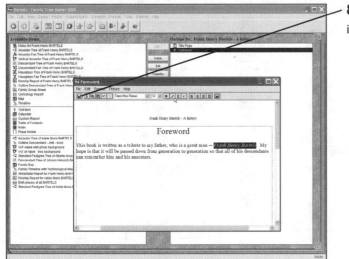

8. Click the **Save** button in the text editing window to save your changes.

9. Click the little X to close the editing window. If you forget to save, a Family Tree Maker dialog box will appear, asking if you want to save changes. Click **Yes** to save your changes. The dialog box will close.

Adding Trees and Reports

You can include several different trees and reports in your book. Make your selections based on the audience who will receive the book. For example, you may want to share more personal and informal trees and reports with family, but you will likely want to remove information about living relatives when sharing your family tree with other genealogists.

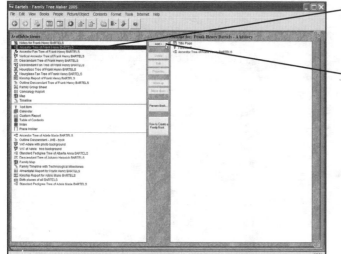

1. Click on the tree or report you want to include in the Available items field. The tree or report will be highlighted.

2. Click **Add>**. The tree or report will be added to the Outline for the list.

TIP

Select as many trees or reports as you would like. You can also double-click on a report instead of clicking the Add> button. You will learn how to organize your selections later in this chapter.

---

3. Click on **Genealogy Report**.

4. Click **Add>**. The Add Genealogy Report dialog box will open.

5. Click in the radio button for the type of Genealogy Report you would like to add. The option will be selected.

6. Click on **OK**. The Add Genealogy Report dialog box will close and the Genealogy Report will appear in the **Outline for** list.

Organizing Selected Items

The items in the **Outline for** list have been added in the order they were selected, and will also be printed in that order. However, you can change that order, and also decide where you would like new chapters in your book to begin.

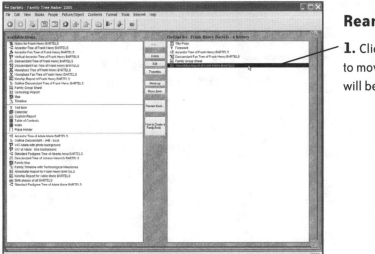

Rearranging the Outline

1. Click on the tree or report you want to move in the **Outline for** list. The item will be highlighted.

2. Click on the **Move up** or **Move down** button to move the highlighted item up or down the outline list.

NOTE

You can also move items in the **Outline for** list by clicking on the item with the left mouse button, and dragging the highlighted item to where you would like it to be on the outline. When you let go of the button, the item will be placed in the new location.

NOTE

The Title Page must remain the first item on the list and the Index page must remain the last item on the list.

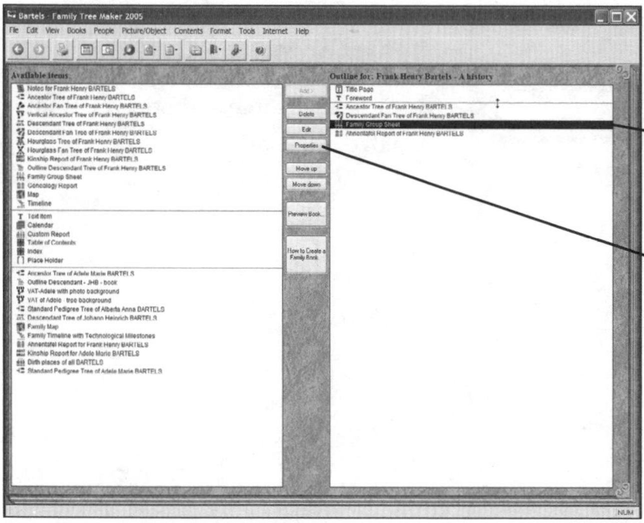

Using the Item Properties Dialog Box

1. Click on a report or tree in the **Outline for** field. The report or tree will be highlighted.

2. Click on the **Properties** button. The Item Properties dialog box will open.

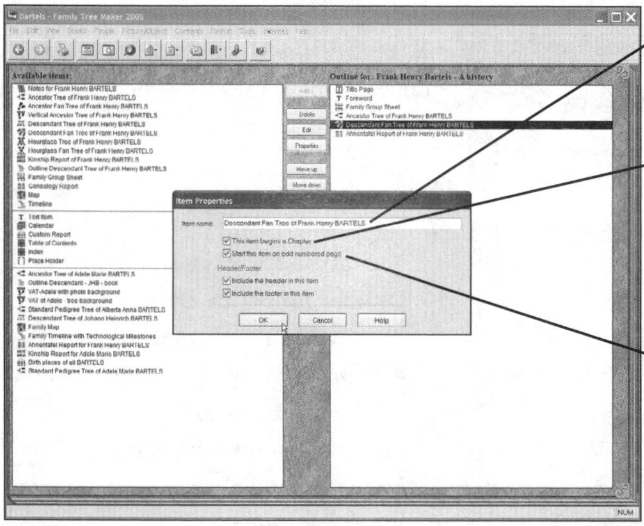

3. Click in the **Item Name** field to type and rename the chart or tree in the book.

4. Click in the **This item begins a Chapter** check box if a check mark does not already exist. If there is already a check mark in the check box, you will deselect it if you click on it.

5. Click the **Start this item on odd numbered page** check box if you want to control on what page this item will begin. A check mark will appear in the check box.

6. Click the **Header/Footer** options if you want the headers and footers to appear on the page.

> ### TIP
>
> The Header is usually the title of the book. The footer is usually the page number.

7. Click on **OK**. Your changes will be saved and the Item Properties dialog box will close.

Renaming Outline Items

You can rename the items in your Book outline if you desire.

1. Click on the appropriate item in the **Outline for** list. The item will be highlighted.

2. Click on the **Properties** button. The Item Properties dialog box will open.

3. Highlight the name in the field and press the **Backspace** or **Delete** button on your keyboard. The text will be deleted.

4. Type the new name in the **Item name** field. This will replace the old item name.

5. Click on **OK**. The Item Properties dialog box will close and the item name will change in the **Outline for** list.

Adding Place Holders

You can use a place holder to reserve a set number of pages anywhere in your book.

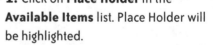

TIP

Place holders are especially helpful if you plan to incorporate a story, chart, photo, etc. from somewhere outside of Family Tree Maker.

1. Click on **Place Holder** in the **Available Items** list. Place Holder will be highlighted.

2. Click on the **Add>** button. The Place Holder dialog box will open.

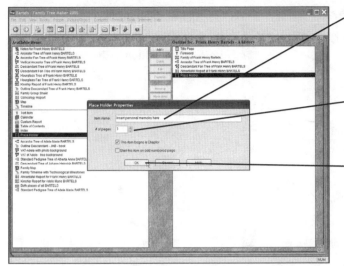

3. Type the name of the item in the **Item name** field. The words **Place Holder** will be replaced with the name you have typed.

4. Click on the up or down arrows for **# of Pages** to select the number of pages to hold.

5. Click on **OK**. The Place Holder Properties dialog box will close.

TIP

You will want to give the place holder a descriptive name so that you can easily recall what will go into those pages. This item name will be displayed in the **Outline for** list, and unlike in the other reports, you cannot open this item to refresh your memory, so you should be clear enough that you will not need a reminder.

Adding Additional Text

You can add additional text to your book that you have not entered anywhere else in your Family File.

1. Click on **Text Item** in the Available Items list. The item will be selected.

2. Click **Add>**. The Add text item dialog box will open.

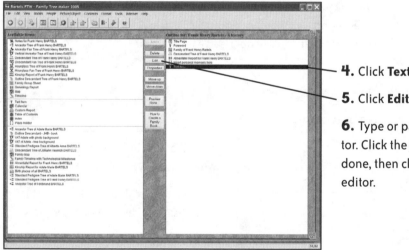

3. Click in the **New Text** radio button if it is not already selected. Click **OK**. The item will be added to the outline.

4. Click **Text Item** from the Outline.

5. Click **Edit**. The Text editor will open.

6. Type or paste text into the text editor. Click the **save** button when you are done, then click **X** to close the file text editor.

Working with Images

Although you have already learned that you can add images to trees and reports before you even select them for your book, you can also add images to a text item and then incorporate the text item into your book.

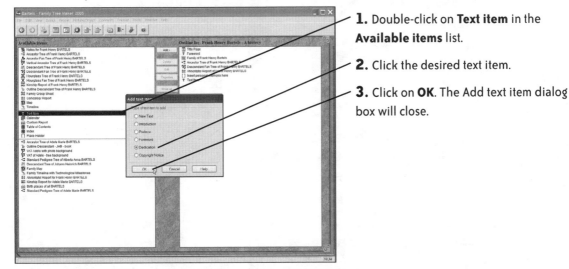

1. Double-click on **Text item** in the **Available items** list.

2. Click the desired text item.

3. Click on **OK**. The Add text item dialog box will close.

4. Click on the newly added text item in the **Outline for** list. The additional option buttons in the center column will be activated so you can move to the next step.

5. Click on **Edit**. The Text Item edit window will open.

6. Click on **Picture**. The Picture menu will appear.

7. Click on **Insert from Scrapbook**. The Individuals with Scrapbook Pictures dialog box will open.

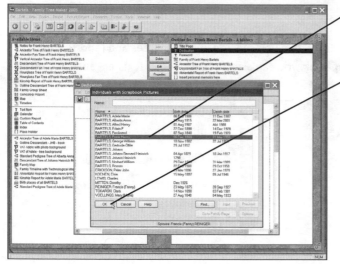

8. Click on the individual whose scrapbook you want to access. The individual will be highlighted.

9. Click on **OK**. The Insert Scrapbook Picture dialog box will open.

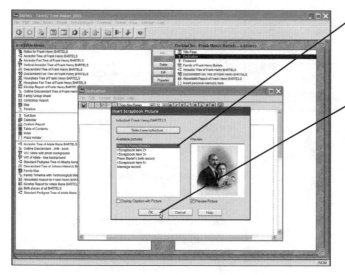

10. Click on the image you would like from the **Available pictures** field. The picture you chose will show in the Preview window.

11. Click **OK** if the picture in the Preview window is the one you expected. The dialog box will close and the picture will be displayed in the text edit window. You can also click **Select new individual** if you want to choose a different picture than the one in the Preview window.

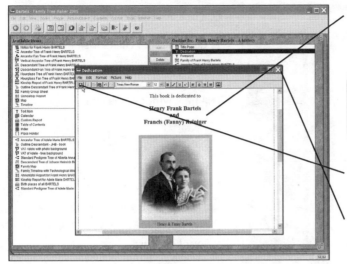

12. Type the text you want to associate with the image in the text edit dialog box.

13. Click on the **Save** button. The changes to the text item will be saved.

14. Click on the **X** or click **Close** from the File menu. The Text Item window will close.

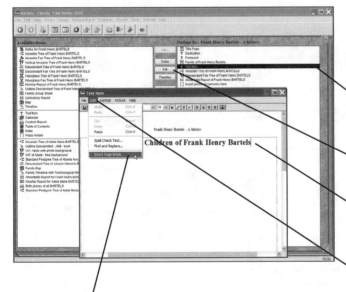

Adding Page Breaks

You can separate your text onto individual pages.

1. Click on the text item you want to edit from the **Outline for** column. The text item will be highlighted.

2. Click on the **Edit** button. The Text Item window will appear.

3. Click where you want to place your page break. The cursor indicator will show where you have clicked.

4. Click on **Edit**. The Edit menu will appear.

5. Click on **Insert Page Break**. A new page will be added in the Text Item window.

6. Click the **Save** button.

7. Click the **X** or click **Close** from the File menu. Family Tree Maker will prompt you to save the changes and the Text Item window will close.

> **TIP**
>
> You can undo the page break by clicking at the front of the text of the new page you have created and pressing the **Backspace** button on your keyboard.

Creating an Index

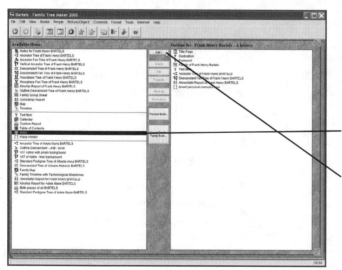

Family Tree Maker automatically creates an index for you as long as you select it for your outline. In addition, you can customize how the index will appear.

1. Click **Index** in the Available items field. The Index will be highlighted.

2. Click **Add**. The Index will be moved to the **Outline for** field.

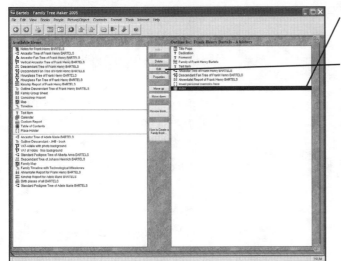

3. In the **Outline for** list, click on **Index**. The Index will be highlighted.

4. Click on **Edit**. The Index of Individuals Report will appear.

5. Click on **Contents**. The Contents menu will appear.

6. Click on **Options**. The Options for Book Index dialog box will open.

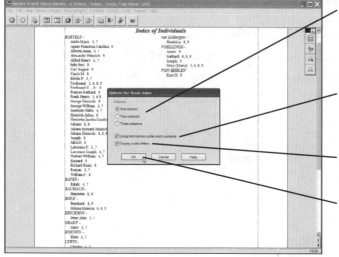

7. Click on the radio button next to the number of columns you would like to see in your index. The option will be selected.

8. Click on the check box **for Group first names under each surname** option. A check mark will appear.

9. Click on the box for **Display index letters**.

10. Click on **OK**. Family Tree Maker will make the requested changes to the report.

TIP

If you do not like the changes you have made, follow steps 3-10 again, selecting and deselecting boxes and radio buttons.

Adding to a Book

After you have created a book and saved it, you can add additional reports or make changes at a later time. Once you have created a book, the book is saved to your Family File.

Adding Saved Reports to Books

1. Click on **Books**. The Books menu will appear.

2. Click on **Open Book**. The Open Book dialog box will appear.

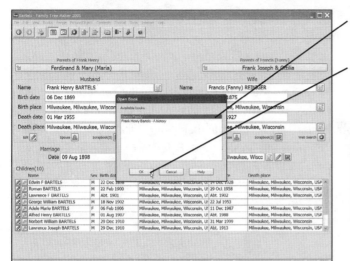

3. Click on the appropriate book. The book will be highlighted.

4. Click on **OK**. The Open Book dialog box will close and the Book view will open.

> **NOTE**
>
> The previously saved reports will always appear at the bottom of the Available Items list.

5. Click on the appropriate saved report from the **Available Items** list. The report will be highlighted.

6. Click on the **Add>** button. The report will be added to the **Outline for** list.

TIP

Although Family Tree Maker uses the name of the main individual in the title of many charts and reports, some of the charts and reports have generic names, e.g., Family Group Sheet. You may want to rename the chart or report to better represent who is included in your report. To do this, go to the report, click on the **Contents** menu and then click **Title & Footnote**. In the Title & Footnote dialog box, click the **Custom title** radio button and then type the new title in the field. Refer to Chapter 10, Creating Specialty and Custom reports, for additional help.

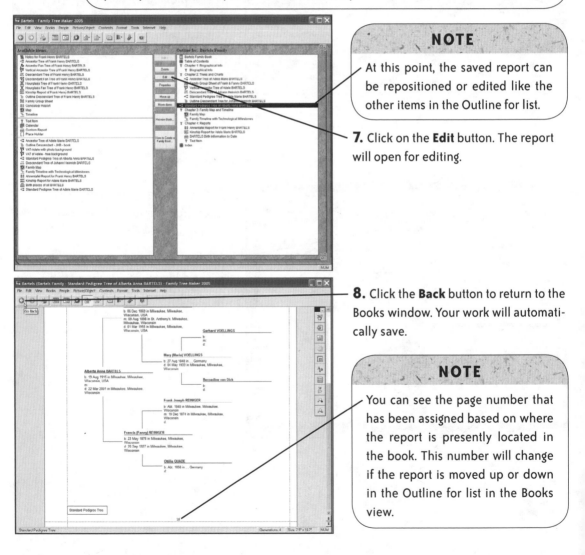

NOTE

At this point, the saved report can be repositioned or edited like the other items in the Outline for list.

7. Click on the **Edit** button. The report will open for editing.

8. Click the **Back** button to return to the Books window. Your work will automatically save.

NOTE

You can see the page number that has been assigned based on where the report is presently located in the book. This number will change if the report is moved up or down in the Outline for list in the Books view.

Adding Reports about Other Individuals

When a book is first created, it relies on the reports of the selected individuals. Once a book has been saved, though, you can add additional reports about other people, giving you a lot of flexibility in your book and its layout.

1. Click **the Index of Individuals** button. The Index of Individual dialog box will open.

TIP

You can also press the F2 key to open the Index of Individuals dialog box.

2. Click on the desired individual. The individual will be highlighted.

3. Click on **OK**. The Index of Individuals dialog box will close and the **Available items** list in the Books view will reflect the change in individual.

4. Click on the appropriate item in the **Available Items** list. That item will be highlighted.

5. Click on the **Add>** button. The selected item will be added to the bottom of the **Outline for** list, just above the **Index** item.

TIP

If you click on the selected item in the **Outline for** list, you can use the various buttons to reposition the item, edit it, or change its properties. It is now part of the book unless you elect to delete the item.

NOTE

Notice that while you changed the focus of the individual in the **Available Items** list, your saved reports are still available.

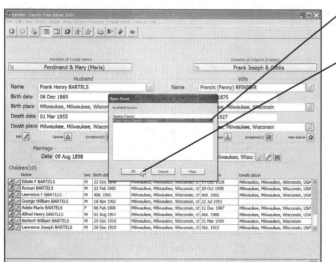

Adding Notes to Books

If you have spent time adding notes about the individuals in your Family File, there will be times when you will want to include the notes in your book, especially when sharing with family members.

1. Click on **Books**. The Books menu will appear.

2. Click on **Open Book**. The Open Book dialog box will open.

3. Click on the appropriate book. The book will be highlighted.

4. Click on **OK**. The Open Book dialog box will close and the Book window will open.

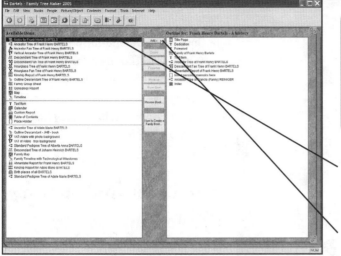

5. Click on **Notes for** in the Available items list. The Notes for item will be selected.

6. Click on the **Add>** button. A message will appear.

7. Click on **OK**. The message box will close and the Notes will be added to the **Outline for** list of items to be included in the book.

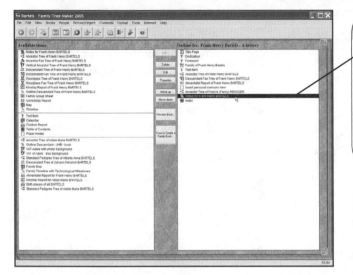

Finalizing and Sharing Your Book

There are several ways to share your book with others. You can print copies to distribute, share the book on a CD-ROM, or even send it via e-mail.

Previewing Your Book

You can preview the final version of your book before printing or sending the book to others.

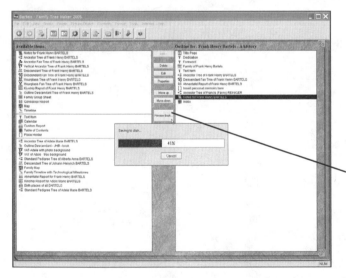

1. Click on **Preview Book**. A dialog box will pop open that says, **Saving to disk ...**, and a blue bar will indicate that Family Tree Maker is in the process of saving your book for preview. Next, a Family Tree Maker 2005 dialog box will open, that says **Processing** across the top. A couple other Family Tree Maker dialog boxes will open and close as Family Tree Maker prepares the document for previewing. The Family Tree Maker book will open in Adobe Reader as a PDF file.

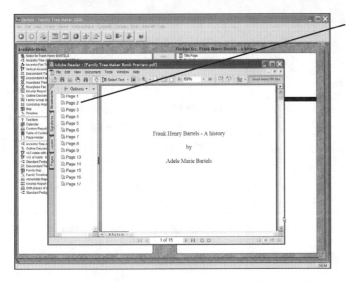

2. Click on each link in the Bookmarks pane to move from page to page.

> ## NOTE
>
> The PDF may open on your com-
> puter but remain minimized. If you
> see a new label at the bottom of
> your screen, typically which reads,
> **Adobe Reader**, click on it to bring
> up the PDF file.

Printing Your Book

You can print your book from the Book page of Family Tree Maker or by pressing the print button in the PDF file you are previewing.

To print from the Book page of Family Tree Maker:

1. Press the **Print** button. The Print Book dialog box will appear.

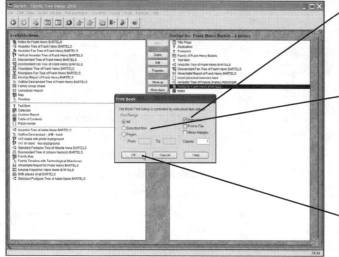

2. Click in the **Print color** box if you want to print in color. If you are printing in black and white, you can uncheck the box.

3. Click in the **All** radio button if you want to print the entire book, or click **Selected Item** to print only the item you have clicked on, or click **Pages** and enter the page numbers of the book that you want to print.

4. Click **OK**. The book will print.

NOTE

You can print more than one book at a time. Change copies from 1 to the number of copies of the book you would like to make. You may prefer to print just one copy of the book and then photocopy the rest to save on time and wear on your printer.

Exporting to PDF

After previewing your book you can save it to your computer for future reference or to send via e-mail. You can also export your book as a PDF directly without previewing:

1. Click on **File**. The File menu will appear.

2. Select **Export Book**. The Export book submenu will appear.

3. Click on **To Acrobat (PDF)**. The Export Books dialog box will open.

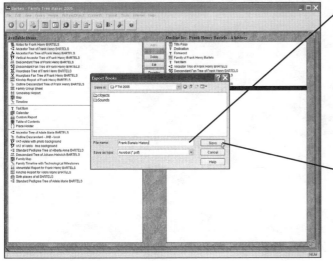

4. Type the name with which you would like to save this file.

5. Click on the **Save** button. The book will be saved.

14

Creating Your Personal Family Tree Maker Home Page

While publishing a family history is sill traditionally done by putting your research on paper, the Internet provides a new way for people to publish their family histories. When publishing to paper, people tend to delay publishing until everything is "perfect." The Internet saves people from this need to delay, as they can always upload a revised version of their pages. In this chapter, you'll learn how to:

- Create a home page

- Add charts, reports, and books to your home page

- Add photographs to your home page

- Remove items from your home page

Creating Your First Home Page

Family Tree Maker makes it easy for you to create your own home page on the Internet. Your Family Home Page will include your own personal touches, a list of all surnames and photos, an index of everyone you choose to include, up to five reports or charts, and an interactive pedigree tree. You will be able to view and share your Family Home Page on Genealogy.com. To create, edit, and view your Family Home Page use the **Internet** menu tools in Family Tree Maker.

1. Click on **Internet**. The Internet menu will appear.

2. Click **Create a Family Home Page**. The Family Home Page dialog box will open.

3. Read the summary about Family Home Pages, then press **Next**. The Individuals to Include page will appear.

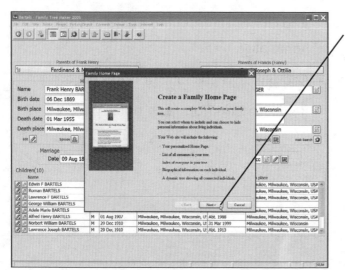

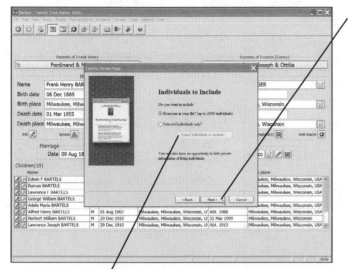

4. Click **Next** to include everyone in your Family Home Page. The Pictures page will appear.

NOTE

If you want to select specific individuals to include in your Family Home Page, choose **Selected individuals only?** The **Select Individuals to Include** button will be activated, and you can click the button to open the Individuals to Include dialog box, which you learned about in earlier chapters, including Chapter 10. Refer to the index for a specific page number. If you are concerned about publishing names of living individuals, you do not have to hand select Individuals to Include. Family Tree Maker gives the option to hide living individuals before publishing.

5. Click the **Include preferred Scrapbook pictures** radio button if you have images you want to share on your Family Home Page. Click **Next**. The Hide Info on Living Individuals page will appear.

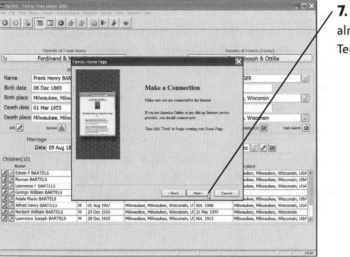

6. Click the **Hide info on Living Individuals** check box. A check mark will appear. Click **Next**. The Make a Connection page will appear.

> ### TIP
>
> While you have the choice to include living individuals, clicking this box is highly recommended to protect the privacy of living individuals.

7. Log onto the Internet if you are not already connected, then click **Next**. The Terms of Service dialog box will open.

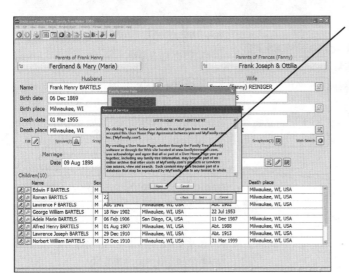

8. Read the Terms of Service. Click **I Agree**. The Terms of Service dialog box will close. The Family Home Page dialog box will say, "Home Page is Building ..." When the Family Home Page is done building, a Family Tree Maker dialog box will appear to inform you that your information has been uploaded. Click **OK** to close the message box.

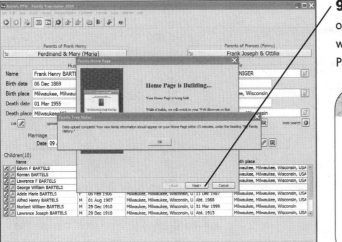

9. Click **Next**. Your Web browser will open to your new home page location, which reads "Create Your Own Home Page."

> ### NOTE
>
> If you have never visited Genealogy.com, or if you have deleted your cookies, you will see a registration page before you see your new home page. You will be prompted through the registration process.

Enhance Your Homepage

1. Click the **Title** field in your Create Your Own Home Page Web page, and type the name you want to appear at the top of your home page.

2. Click on the **Do not include my name on my home page** box. The check mark will appear and your name will not be included on the Web page or leave the **Do not include my name on my home page** box empty.

3. Click in the **First Name** field of the **Contact information** section.

4. Type your first name. Press the **Tab** key to move to the next field.

5. Continue to supply information in the Contact Information section using the Tab key to move to the next field.

NOTE

This Web page will be longer than your computer screen. You may want to use the scroll bar to the right to move up and down the page. The screen shots depicted here do not show the full length of the Web page.

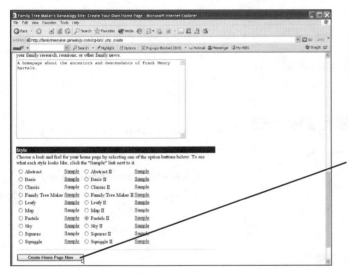

6. Describe your website in the **Text** box and then press the **Tab** key. The cursor will move to the Style section.

TIP

You are more likely to have visitors that you can learn from and who will learn from you if you provide a clear description of your research, what your purpose is, and introduce visitors to your site.

---

7. Click in a radio button to choose a Style for your Web page.

TIP

Click on the Sample link next to each style for an example of how it will look. Then, use the back button on your browser to return to making your own selection.

---

8. Click on the **Create Home Page Now** button. The page will be created and shown in your browser.

Adding Charts, Reports, and Books to Your Home Page

After you upload your family tree you can continually enhance it by adding additional reports or even a book. You can always update your tree.

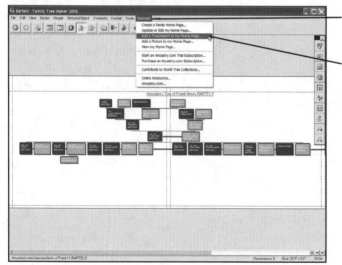

Adding Charts and Reports

1. Click on the **tree charts** button or the **reports** button, then click a tree or a report that you want to appear on your home page. The report will appear.

2. Click on **Internet**. The Internet menu will appear.

3. Click **Add a Tree/Report to my Home Page**. The Add a Tree or Report to your Home Page dialog box will appear.

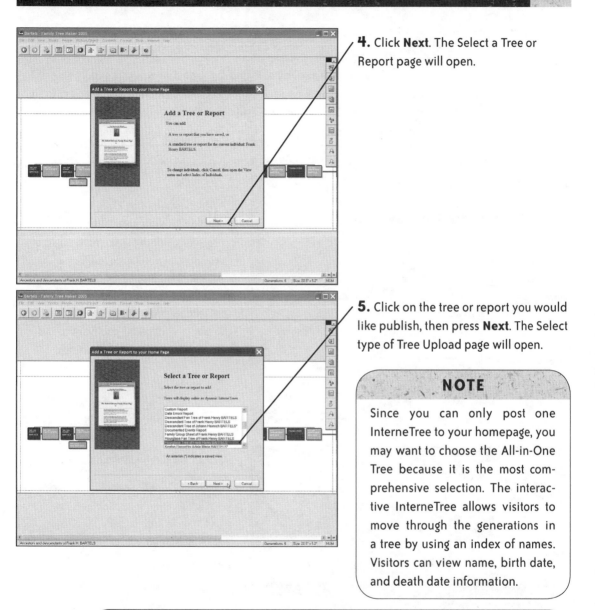

4. Click **Next**. The Select a Tree or Report page will open.

5. Click on the tree or report you would like publish, then press **Next**. The Select type of Tree Upload page will open.

NOTE

Since you can only post one InterneTree to your homepage, you may want to choose the All-in-One Tree because it is the most comprehensive selection. The interactive InterneTree allows visitors to move through the generations in a tree by using an index of names. Visitors can view name, birth date, and death date information.

TIP

The InterneTree can hold up to 2,000 individuals. This is important to remember if you have chosen to upload a report that includes all the individuals in your database.

> ## NOTE
>
> Family Tree Maker should have already selected the tree that was opened. If you still want to publish that tree, you only need to check to make sure that it is selected, then click Next. Or, use the scroll bar to move up and down the menu, then click on the new tree you would like to publish.

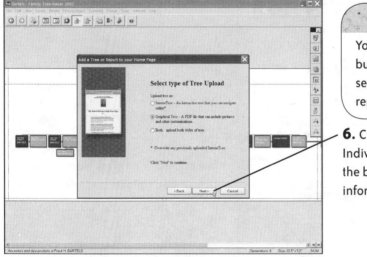

> ## TIP
>
> You may need to click the Refresh button in your Internet browser to see the InterneTree in the list of reports on your homepage.

6. Click **Next**. The Hide Info on Living Individuals page will open. Make sure the box is checked if you want to hide information on living individuals.

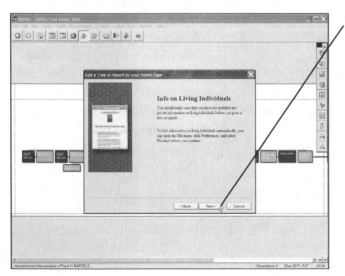

7. Click **Next**. The Make a Connection page will open.

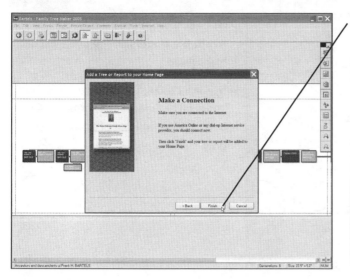

8. Make sure you are connected to the Internet, then click **Finish**. Family Tree Maker will pop open a dialog box to let you know your chart or report has successfully uploaded and will be linked to your Home Page and available within 15 minutes.

> **TIP**
>
> As you learned earlier in this chapter, you can view changes to your home page. Click on the **Internet** menu, then **View my Home Page**.

Adding a Book

You can add your family book to your home page. If you update your book, you can simply upload a new version of the book to your home page.

1. Click **Books**. The Books menu will open.

2. Click **Publish a Book to Your Home Page**. The Select Book to Upload dialog box will open.

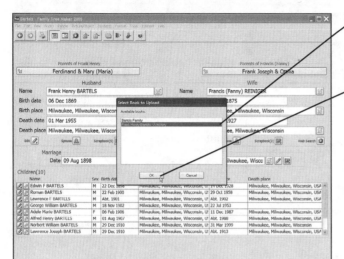

3. Click the book you want from the **Available books** list. The book will be highlighted.

4. Click on **OK**. The Book window will appear. The Select Book Format dialog box will open in front of the Book window.

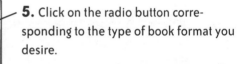

5. Click on the radio button corresponding to the type of book format you desire.

6. Click **OK**. A Book Upload dialog box will open.

> ### NOTE
>
> You may see a few different dialog boxes with short instructions or questions. If you have left required items out of your book, Family Tree Maker will ask you if it is okay to add the mandatory items. Click **Yes** or **OK**. In addition, you may be asked if you want to contribute to the World Tree Collections project. This is a set of user-submitted family tree collections compiled by MyFamily.com, Inc., for researchers interested in sharing their information.

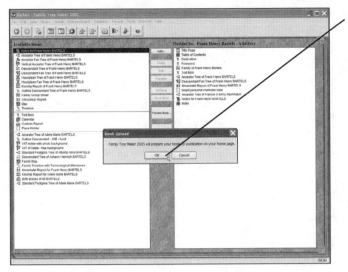

7. Click **OK**. The Saving to disk dialog box will open as Family Tree Maker prepares to save the book to the Internet. Then, a dialog box will open to tell you when you have successfully posted to the Web.

> ### NOTE
>
> You can only have one book uploaded to your home page at a time. If you upload a new book, it will replace the existing book.

Adding Photographs to your Home Page

1. Click **Add a Picture to My Home Page** from the **Internet** menu. The Individuals with Scrapbook Pictures dialog box will open.

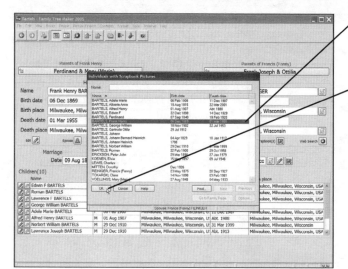

2. Click an individual from the Individuals with Scrapbook Pictures dialog box.

3. Click **OK**. The dialog box will close and the Insert Scrapbook Picture dialog box will open.

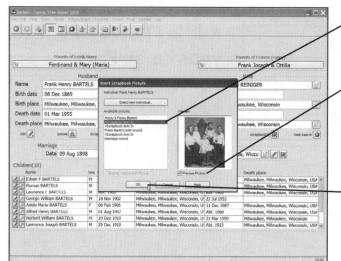

4. Click a picture from the **Available pictures** box. The picture name will be selected.

5. Click the **Preview Picture** check box if a preview picture is not showing. A check will be added to the box indicating it has been selected, and a picture will appear.

6. Click **OK**. The Title and Description dialog box will open.

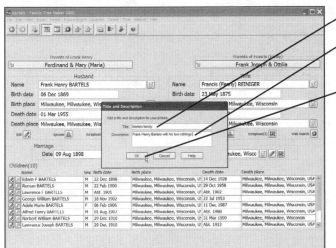

7. Click in the **title field** and type a title.

8. Click in the **Description field** and type a description.

9. Click **OK**. A message will appear indicating that you have successfully posted to your Home Page.

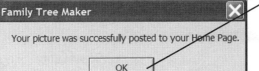

10. Click **OK**.

NOTE

You can upload any photos on your computer to your homepage, even if the photo is not in your scrapbook, by uploading directly from the Web page.

Removing Items from your Home Page

You can remove items from your Home Page if you no longer want them online.

1. Click on **Internet**. The Internet menu will open.

2. Click **View my Home Page**. Your Internet Home Page will open.

3. Click on **Edit Your Page**. The Author Options page will open in your browser.

4. Scroll to the **Remove Information** section at the bottom of the edit page and click on the link for the information you want to remove. The Removing page will appear.

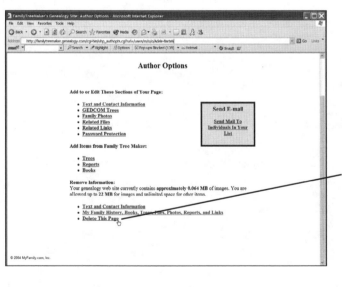

5. Click on the check box next to the item you wish to remove. A check mark will appear.

6. Click **Removed Selected Items**. The item(s) will be removed.

Deleting Your Home Page

If you would prefer to delete your entire home page, you may do so. You can always re-create your home page at a later date.

1. Follow steps 1-3 above (Removing Items from your Home Page.)

2. Scroll to the Remove Information section at the bottom of the edit page and click on **Delete This Page**. Your home page will be deleted. All reports and trees you have created will no longer be online.

15

Working with Other Family Files

At some point in your research you may receive a database from another researcher, or you may want to share your research with somebody else. Such sharing is usually done through the GEDCOM (GEnealogical Data COMmunications) computer file format. There will also be times when you will want to keep some of your research in a separate Family File, or compare two files. In this chapter, you'll learn how to:

- Export all or part of your Family File
- Import a GEDCOM file to an existing Family File
- Open two Family Files to compare
- Merge data between files
- Save a backup of your Family File

You may want to share a Family File with another researcher, or import or merge another individual's Family File with your own file. Family Tree Maker allows for many file merging and sharing scenarios.

Exporting All or Part of Your Family File

GEDCOM is the standard file format used to transfer data between different genealogy software packages. When you share your file with others, you will likely use the GEDCOM format. To save a copy of your file as a GEDCOM, first make sure you are in Family View.

1. Click on **File**. The File menu will appear.

2. Select **Export File**. A fly-out menu will appear.

3. Click on **Entire File**.

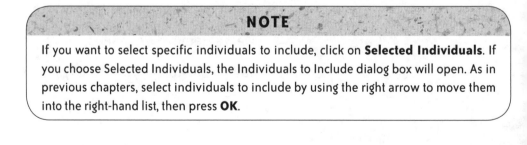

> ### NOTE
>
> While Family Tree Maker allows you to add digitized images, sounds, and objects, these items will not be included in the GEDCOM file.

> ### NOTE
>
> If you want to select specific individuals to include, click on **Selected Individuals**. If you choose Selected Individuals, the Individuals to Include dialog box will open. As in previous chapters, select individuals to include by using the right arrow to move them into the right-hand list, then press **OK**.

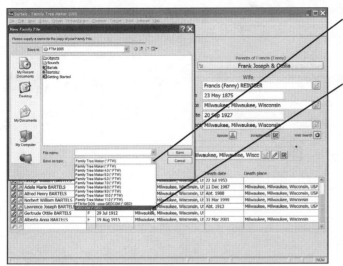

4. Click on the **Save as type** down arrow. The Save as type menu will appear.

5. Click on **GEDCOM (*.GED).** The GEDCOM option will be selected.

NOTE

Family Tree Maker automatically names the GEDCOM file with the same name as the Family File. You can double-click on this name to highlight it and type a new name. Make sure the file extension ends in GED, for example, SmithFamily.GED.

TIP

Make a note of where the file is saved, so you can find it later.

6. Click on the **Save** button. The Export to GEDCOM dialog box will open.

NOTE

The default settings for exporting your GEDCOM file are usually correct. However, if you are a Latter-day Saint creating a file for TempleReady, you will want to use the Destination drop-down menu to select TempleReady.

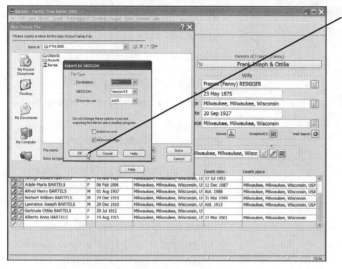

7. Click on **OK**. The Export to GEDCOM dialog box will close and the file will be saved.

Working with Older Versions of Family Tree Maker Family Files

You cannot open Family Tree Maker 2005 files in older versions of Family Tree Maker. However, you can save a copy of your Family Tree Maker 2005 file that is compatible with an older version of Family Tree Maker if you want to share your file with someone who does not have the latest version.

1. Open the Family File you want to share.

2. Click on **File**. The File menu will open.

3. Select **Export File**. A fly-out menu will appear.

4. Click on **Enter File**. The New Family File dialog box will open.

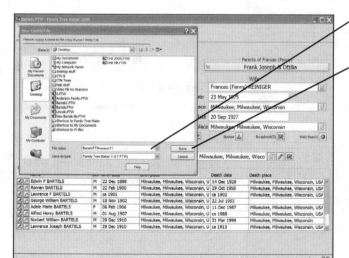

5. Click the **Save as type** drop-down arrow. The drop-down menu will appear.

6. Click on the desired version of Family Tree Maker. The menu will close and your selection will appear in the **Save as type** field.

7. Click in the **File name** field and type what you would like to name the file.

8. Click **Save**. The new version will be saved to the designated file. You can then save this version to a disk or e-mail it so they can open it in their older version of Family Tree Maker.

NOTE

Once you save a file as in older version of FTM, do not open it in FTM 2005, or it will re-save the program as an FTM 2005 file.

Importing a GEDCOM File to an Existing Family File

You can import a GEDCOM file directly into your Family File.

1. Click on **File**. The File menu will open.

2. Click on **Append/Merge**. A dialog box will ask you if you wish to create a backup. It is a good idea to backup your file on a regular basis, and especially before any major alteration. Click **Yes** to back up, or click **no** to skip to the next step. The dialog box will close and the Select File to Merge or Append dialog box will open.

> ## NOTE
>
> To create a backup, click **Yes**. Select where you would like to save your Family File, then click **OK**. Family Tree Maker will back up your file and alert you that the backup was successful. Click **OK** when the dialog box opens. Then, click **Yes** to return to the merge process.

> ## TIP
>
> Save a new GEDCOM as a separate Family File first. This allows you to evaluate the data before it gets mixed in your own Family File. Once you have determined its accuracy, you can then follow the steps described here to add this file to your personal Family File.

3. Click the Files of type drop down arrow and click GEDCOM (*.GED). Click the GEDCOM file you'd like to merge or append. The file name will be highlighted and will appear in the **File** name field. Then click **OK**. The Import from GEDCOM dialog box will open.

TIP

If you cannot find the GEDCOM file in the list of names, you may be looking in the wrong location. Click the drop-down arrow for **Look in** to select where you may have saved the item.

4. Click **Facts to Import** from GEDCOM dialog box. The Facts to Import dialog box will open.

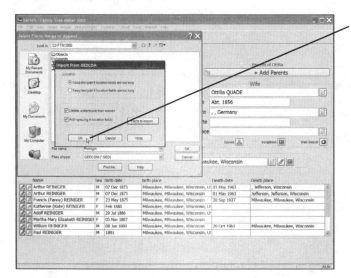

5. Scan through the list and make sure you agree with where Family Tree Maker wants to put some of the facts that will be imported.

6. Click on **OK**. The Facts to Import dialog box will close.

7. Click on **OK**. The Import from GEDCOM dialog box will close, the GEDCOM file will be appended to the Family File, and a message box will open stating your merge was successful.

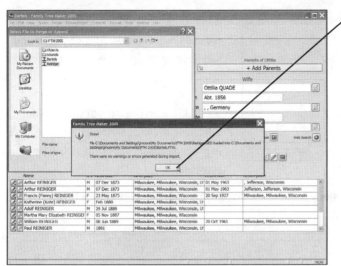

8. Click on **OK**. The message box will close and the Individuals to Include dialog box will open.

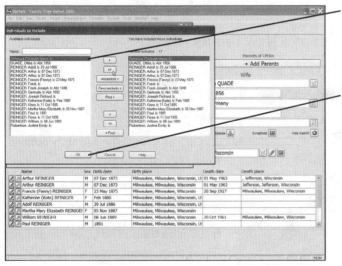

9. Click on an individual you want to add from the **Available individuals** list, then click the **>** button to move the individual to the right column.

10. Click on **OK**. The Append File dialog box will open.

11a. Click on the **Continue and merge records** radio button. The continue and merge records option will be selected.

Or

11b. Click on the **Do not merge, just add new records without merging** radio button. This option will be selected.

12. Click on **Continue**. The Likely Matches dialog box or a force merge dialog box will open depending on which option you chose.

TIP

If you need a refresher on how to check the Family File for duplicate individuals, see Chapter 4, "Editing Information about a Family."

Opening a GEDCOM Files as a New Family File

You can use a GEDCOM file to create a new Family File.

1. Click on **File**. The File menu will appear.

2. Click on **Close**. The currently opened Family File will close.

3. Click on **File**. The File menu will appear.

4. Click on **Open**. The Open Family File dialog box will open.

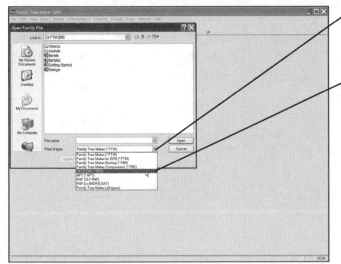

5. Click on the **Files of type** down arrow. The Files of type menu will appear.

6. Click on **GEDCOM (*.GED)**. The GEDCOM file type will be selected.

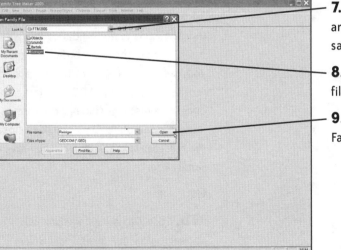

7. Click on the **Look in** drop-down arrow and make sure your file will be saved to the correct location.

8. Click on the appropriate GEDCOM file. The file will be selected.

9. Click on the **Open** button. The New Family File dialog box will open.

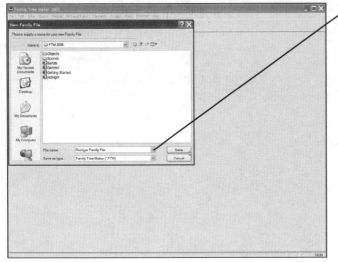

10. Type a new name for the GEDCOM file into the **File** name field. Click **Save**. The Import from GEDCOM dialog box will open.

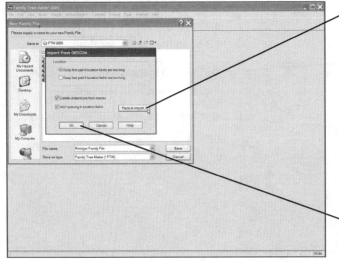

11a. Click on the **Facts to import** button. The Facts to Import dialog box will open. Click in the radio buttons to make your selection, then click **OK** twice, once for the Import from GEDCOM dialog box, once for a message that opens when the import is complete. Click on **OK** to close the message box and go into the new Family File.

Or

11b. Click **OK**. A message box will appear, telling you the import is complete.

Importing a File from Ancestry Family Tree

If you created a Family File in Ancestry Family Tree, you can import the file into Family Tree Maker. Make sure you know where your AFT file is saved on your computer before proceeding with these steps in Family Tree Maker.

1. Click **File**. The File menu will open.

2. Click **Open**. The Open Family File dialog box will open.

3. Click the **Files of type** drop-down arrow. A drop-down menu will appear.

4. Click **AFT (*.AFT)** from the list. All files you have saved as an Ancestry Family Tree in that folder will appear.

NOTE

If the AFT file you want is not in the folder, you will need to select the correct folder by clicking the **Look in** drop-down arrow, then clicking the appropriate folder.

5. Click on the AFT file you want to open. The name will appear in the **File name** field.

6. Click **Open**. The New Family File dialog box will open, with the same file in the File name field, except the extension has changed from .AFT to .FTW.

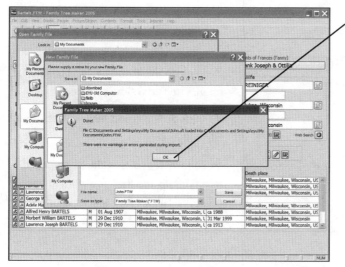

7. Click **Save**. A dialog box will open indicating if you have successfully saved your Ancestry Family Tree file as a Family Tree Maker file.

8. Click **OK**. The dialog boxes will close, and your new Family File will open in Family Tree Maker.

Opening Two Family Files to Compare

You may have more than one Family File. Perhaps your second file is for individuals with the same surname only, or for individuals with whom you do not yet understand the connection. You can have these files open at the same time for easy comparison.

1. Click on **File**. The File menu will appear.

2. Click on **Open**. The Family File dialog box will open.

3. Click on the **Family File** you want to open. The File will be selected.

4. Click on the **Open** button. The Family File will open.

5. Follow steps 1-4 again, but with a different family file that you want to open. A second Family Tree Maker window will open with the new Family File.

Using File History

Family Tree Maker remembers the last four Family Files you have opened, including the one you currently have open. They are listed at the bottom of the file menu. Click on the desired Family File, and it will open.

TIP

When you have two Family Files open, you can copy and paste between the two of them. For more information on how to copy and paste, see Chapter 3.

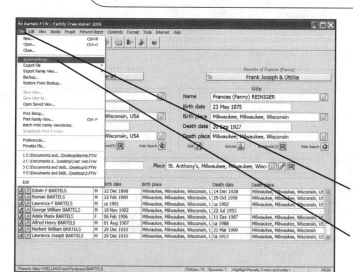

Merging Two Family Files

Rather than simply comparing two Family Files, you can always merge the Family Files. Make sure you have one of the two Family Files open and that you are in the Family View.

1. Click on the **File** menu. The File menu will open.

2. Click **Append/Merge ...** A dialog box will open asking if you want to create a backup of your file.

3. Click **Yes** to create a backup or **No** to skip to the next step. The Select File to Merge or Append dialog box will open.

4. Click on the file you want to merge from the list. You may have to use the **Look in** drop-down arrow to find your file. Once you click on the name, the name will appear in the **File name** field.

5. Click **OK**. The Individuals to Include dialog box will open.

6. Click on the names from the left column and then click on the center buttons to select which individuals you want to move to the Family File you have open.

NOTE

You can find more detailed information on how to use this dialog box in Chapter 5, or you can refer to the Index.

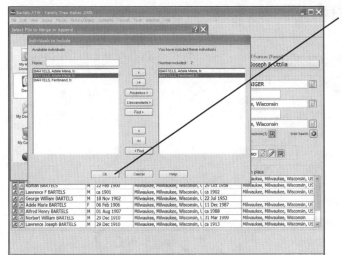

7. Click **OK** when you have finished selecting which individuals to merge into your Family File.

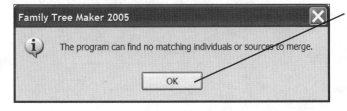

8. Click **OK** if you see a dialog box noting that no additional source information was found. This occurs when Family Tree Maker has found no matching individuals or source information. Family Tree Maker will simply add the individuals, instead of merging them, if this occurs.

9. Click the radio button to select if you want to merge information or add information. Depending on the data, Family Tree Maker may not allow you to perform one of the options.

NOTE

You can click **View/Print Detailed Merge Report** to view the information Family Tree Maker found regarding the merge and what actions Family Tree Maker will take.

10. Click **Continue**. The Merge Sources dialog box will open.

Merge Sources

These two sources appear to be the same:

Field	Source 1	Source 2
Source title	Providence, Rhode Island City Directory, 1887	Providence, Rhode Island City Directory, 1887
Source file	Andersen Family.FTW	Bartels family restored.FTW

Click the option buttons next to the information that you want to keep:

Source Author	⦿ Ancestry.com	○ <EMPTY>
Comment on the Source	○ <EMPTY>	⦿ Online database also has directories from several other years

[Merge] [Don't merge] [Cancel] [Help]

11. Click the radio buttons next to the information that you want to keep. If Family Tree Maker found sources in both files that appear to be the same, it will present them for your confirmation. If the fields have different information, it will ask you to choose which to keep. Sources that are identical will automatically be merged and new sources will automatically be added.

12. Click **Merge**. The Likely Matches dialog box will open. This dialog box will show you a list of likely matches between the two files.

Likely Matches ☒

The 12 individuals listed below are likely but not positive matches. Indicate which you wish to merge.

Merge	Individual to be Merged ---------> Individual in Your File	
☑	Adele Marie BARTELS b. 06 Feb 1906	Adele Marie BARTELS b. 06 Feb 1906	Details...
☑	Ferdinand BARTELS b. 07 Sep 1840	Ferdinand BARTELS b. 07 Sep 1840	Details...
☑	Frank Henry BARTELS b. 06 Dec 1869	Frank Henry BARTELS b. 06 Dec 1869	Details...
☑	Johann BARTELS b. <empty>	Johann BARTELS b. <empty>	Details...
☑	Johann Heinrich BARTELS b. 1798	Johann Heinrich BARTELS b. 1798	Details...
☑	Bernhard BOLK b. <empty>	Bernhard BOLK b. <empty>	Details...
☑	Helena Henrica BOLK b. 1800	Helena Henrica BOLK b. 1800	Details...
☑	Ottilia QUADE b. Abt. 1856	Ottilia QUADE b. Abt. 1856	Details...
☑	Frances (Fanny) REINIGER b. 23 Ma...	Frances (Fanny) REINIGER b. 23 Ma...	Details...

[Select All] [Select None]

* Indicates pairs with conflicting facts. Click "Details" to select facts to keep.

[Merge Selected and Continue] [Cancel] [Help]

13. Click to check or uncheck the boxes. If you remove a checkmark from a checkbox in the left column, you will prevent the merge of the two individuals.

14. Click on the details column to see more information about the individuals to help you make your decision, or skip to step 16.

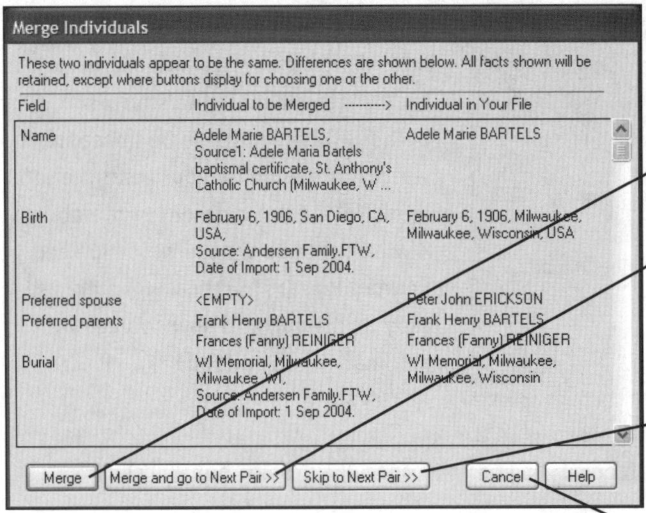

Merge Individuals

These two individuals appear to be the same. Differences are shown below. All facts shown will be retained, except where buttons display for choosing one or the other.

Field	Individual to be Merged ---------->	Individual in Your File
Name	Adele Marie BARTELS, Source1: Adele Maria Bartels baptismal certificate, St. Anthony's Catholic Church (Milwaukee, W ...	Adele Marie BARTELS
Birth	February 6, 1906, San Diego, CA, USA, Source: Andersen Family.FTW, Date of Import: 1 Sep 2004.	February 6, 1906, Milwaukee, Milwaukee, Wisconsin, USA
Preferred spouse	<EMPTY>	Peter John ERICKSON
Preferred parents	Frank Henry BARTELS Frances (Fanny) REINIGER	Frank Henry BARTELS Frances (Fanny) REINIGER
Burial	WI Memorial, Milwaukee, Milwaukee, WI, Source: Andersen Family.FTW, Date of Import: 1 Sep 2004.	WI Memorial, Milwaukee, Milwaukee, Wisconsin

[Merge] [Merge and go to Next Pair >>] [Skip to Next Pair >>] [Cancel] [Help]

15. Click one of the following buttons according to what action you want to perform for the first pair of individuals:

a. Merge – This will merge the two individuals and close the dialog box.

b. Merge and go to the Next Pair – This will merge the individuals but keep the details database open to see the details for the next set of individuals

c. Skip to the Next Pair – This will prevent the merge of these two and move on to the details of the next pair.

d. Cancel – This will close the dialog box and return the information to the list with the check boxes.

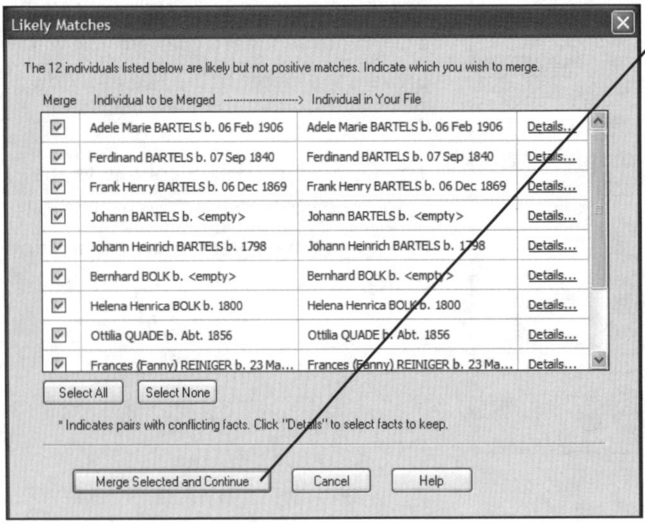

Likely Matches

The 12 individuals listed below are likely but not positive matches. Indicate which you wish to merge.

Merge	Individual to be Merged ----------> Individual in Your File	
☑	Adele Marie BARTELS b. 06 Feb 1906	Adele Marie BARTELS b. 06 Feb 1906	Details...
☑	Ferdinand BARTELS b. 07 Sep 1840	Ferdinand BARTELS b. 07 Sep 1840	Details...
☑	Frank Henry BARTELS b. 06 Dec 1869	Frank Henry BARTELS b. 06 Dec 1869	Details...
☑	Johann BARTELS b. <empty>	Johann BARTELS b. <empty>	Details...
☑	Johann Heinrich BARTELS b. 1798	Johann Heinrich BARTELS b. 1798	Details...
☑	Bernhard BOLK b. <empty>	Bernhard BOLK b. <empty>	Details...
☑	Helena Henrica BOLK b. 1800	Helena Henrica BOLK b. 1800	Details...
☑	Ottilia QUADE b. Abt. 1856	Ottilia QUADE b. Abt. 1856	Details...
☑	Frances (Fanny) REINIGER b. 23 Ma...	Frances (Fanny) REINIGER b. 23 Ma...	Details...

[Select All] [Select None]

* Indicates pairs with conflicting facts. Click "Details" to select facts to keep.

[Merge Selected and Continue] [Cancel] [Help]

16. Click **Merge Selected and Continue** when you have finished making your selections. Your merge will be completed and the dialog box will close.

Family Tree Maker

No matches were found for the 82 individuals listed below. They will be added as new individuals in your file.

If you know that one of them matches an individual already in your file, then select that person and click "Force a Merge."

Unmatched Individual:

John Alexander b. <empty>
Margaret Ellen Alexander b. 29 Jan 1869
William Alexander b. <empty>
William Alexander b. <empty>
William Alexander b. Abt. 1846
Frank Henry BARTELS b. 06 Dec 1869
Johann BARTELS b. <empty>
Johann Heinrich BARTELS b. 1798
Elizabeth Blair b. <empty>
Henry Blair b. <empty>
Margaret Buchanan b. <empty>
Robert Buchanan b. <empty>
Henry Cameron b. <empty>
Mary Cameron b. <empty>
Sarah Cameron b. <empty>
Ellen Casey b. <empty>

[Force a Merge...] [Delete Individual...]

Tip: You can merge individuals in your file anytime using the "Merge Two Specific Individuals" command on the People menu.

[Continue] [Cancel] [Help]

NOTE

If Family Tree Maker could not find any matches for some of the individuals, it will display a list of Unmatched Individuals. Unless you specify otherwise, these people will be added as new individuals to your Family File. You can force a merge with someone in your file if you know they are the same. Click the individual, click on the force merge button, and click the person to merge into from the list of individuals into your file.

NOTE

You can undo the file merge immediately after the merge if you think you made a mistake. If you make any other changes to your file, you cannot undo the merge. To undo the merge immediately, select **Undo** from the **Edit** menu.

Saving a Backup of Your Family File

Earlier in this chapter, you learned how you could save a back up of your Family File in a specific area when Family Tree Maker prompted you. You can also save a backup at any time.

1. Click on the **File** menu. The File menu will open.

2. Click on **Backup**. The Backup Family File dialog box will open.

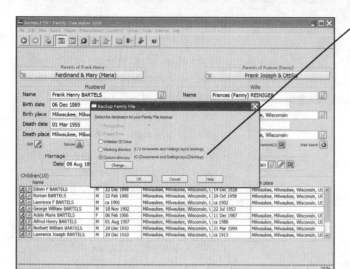

3. Click on the radio button corresponding to the manner in which you would prefer to save your backup.

PART VI

Working with Preferences and Tools

16

Setting Family Tree Maker Preferences

Family Tree Maker is a powerful program that offers many features and options. To help you get the most out of the software, Family Tree Maker allows you to define your preferences for many of the screens and more common activities. In this chapter, you'll learn how to:

- Change general preferences

- Change editing preferences

- Change date preferences

- Change label, titles, and LDS preferences

- Change image preferences

- Change reference number preferences

Family Tree Maker has many standard settings that will allow you to change the way dates are displayed, automatically save your Family File for you as you work, and check for name errors when you enter data. You can change these default settings and many others in the Preferences dialog box.

The Preferences dialog box features six tabs that allow you to locate the preference settings by category: General, Editing, Dates, Labels/Titles/LDS, Images, and Reference Numbers. Simply open the dialog box, then click on the tab to view the preference settings.

To open the Preferences dialog box:

1. Click on the **File** menu.

2. Click **Preferences**. The Preferences dialog box will open.

General Tab

When you open the Preferences dialog box, the dialog box opens the General tab by default (if it does not, click on the **General** tab). Click in the boxes to check or uncheck any of the desired options. If items are not checked, Family Tree Maker will ignore those options. Click **OK** at the bottom of the Preferences dialog box to save your changes. The features of the General tab will be covered by section (General, Pedigree View, Measurement System, and Search).

General Section

• **Automatically backup Family File**—Family Tree Maker saves a copy of your Family File when you exit the program. The backup file has the same name as the original file, but with the extension .FBK. You can use this backup file if your original file is ever lost or damaged. However, since the backup file takes up space on your computer's hard drive, you may want to deselect this option if your computer's hard drive space is limited.

• **Don't allow new files to have same name as existing ones**—Prevents the confusion of having multiple files with the same name and accidentally working in the wrong file.

> **TIP**
>
> It is a good idea to leave both of these options turned on (by leaving the checkmark in the checkbox). This not only creates a backup of your file when exiting the program, but prevents you from overwriting an existing Family File when creating a new Family File.

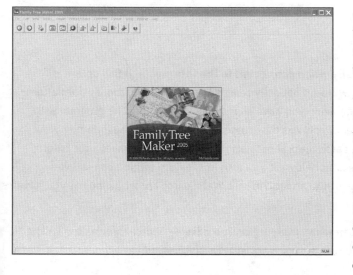

• Automatically check for update when connected to the Internet— When this box is checked, Family Tree Maker will automatically look for updates to Family Tree Maker 2005 and alert you if an update exists.

• Show splash screen — Allows you to choose whether to show the splash screen that automatically appears each time you open Family Tree Maker.

• Use FTM classic colors — Reverts Family Tree Maker 2005 to the classic yellow background used in previous versions of Family Tree Maker. Family Tree Maker 2005 colors are now based on the program colors of your Windows operating system. Selecting this option will also cause the program background color to change to green if you privatize the file or if you make the file a read-only.

Pedigree View Section

• **Number of generations to show** — Click on the drop-down menu to select the default number of generations that appear in Pedigree View. Family Tree Maker allows you to change the number of generations that appear in your Pedigree View chart as well, as discussed in Chapter 5.

• **Enable animation in Pedigree View** — The Pedigree View animation shows names shifting up or down a tree when you select a new primary individual or visit an ancestor or descendant not on the current display. The purpose of this animation is to help you visualize where ancestors are shifted along the tree as you work. When you uncheck this box, you disable this feature.

Measurement System Section

• **Measurement system** — Click the English radio button if you want to use feet, inches, pounds, and ounces. Click the Metric radio button if you prefer to use meters, centimeters, grams, and kilograms.

> **NOTE**
>
> The measurement system setting applies only to the Family File you have open and will not carry over into other files.

Search Section

• **Search online automatically when connected to the Internet** — If this option is checked, Family Tree Maker will automatically search Ancestry.com for more information on the individuals in your file when you have an Internet connection. The program will conduct a search on each person only as they come into your view through Family View, Pedigree View, or the Web Search report and alert you when matches meet your criteria (see Show search result indicator below). If you turn this feature off, you can still view Web Search results by navigating to an individual's Web Search report, as long as you have Internet connectivity.

• **Include source information when merging online data** — Source information will be included when you use Web Merge.

• **Show search result indicator** — Choose when Family Tree Maker will indicate that a Web Search result meets your criteria. If a Web Search result matches the quality level you set, the Web Search icon will change to include a gold star in both the Family and Pedigree Views. The higher the number of stars, the more likely the match will be relevant, but setting too high of a threshold may also cause you to miss relevant information.

• **When searching CDs, include Soundex matches** — If this option is clicked, Family Tree Maker searches for Soundex results, which help you find matches where the name could be the same but the spelling is different Spelling differences could arise from translation errors, for example, spelling "Smith" as "Smythe."

> **NOTE**
>
> These settings apply only to the Family File you have open and will not carry over into other files.

Customize Toolbar Button

Click the **Customize Toolbar** button to go to the Customize Toolbar dialog box.

The default toolbar buttons are listed in the right column. You can add additional buttons to the toolbar (listed in the left column), change the order of the buttons, and add separators to show spaces between buttons.

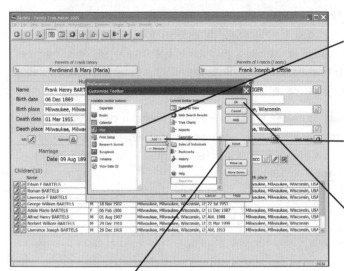

To customize your toolbar:

1. Click on the item you would like to add to the toolbar from the **Available toolbar buttons** list. The item will be highlighted to show that it has been selected.

2. Click the **Add**-> button. The item will be moved to the **Current toolbar buttons** list.

3. Click an item you want to remove from the **Current toolbar buttons** list and click **Remove**, or press **OK** to save your changes.

NOTE

You can click the **Reset** button if you want to return the toolbar to its default setting.

Editing Tab

Click on the Editing tab of the Preferences dialog box to view and change your Editing Preferences options. Click in the boxes to check or uncheck any of the desired options. Family Tree Maker will ignore items that are not checked. Click OK at the bottom of the Preferences dialog box to save your changes. The features of the Editing tab will be covered by section (Errors to check during data entry, Spell Check, Navigation, Use Fastfields for, and Edit Individual/Marriage fact columns).

> **NOTE**
>
> If you change the preference for any item in the Editing tab, except the Spell Check features and the Edit Individual/Marriage Facts column, the preference selection will apply only to the current Family File and will not carry over into other files. You will need to make this selection again for other Family Files.

Errors to Check during Data Entry

• **Name errors** — Include a checkmark in the checkbox if you want Family Tree Maker to warn you when you enter names that do not look right (for example, names that include numbers).

• **Unlikely birth, death & marriage dates** — Include a checkmark in the checkbox if Family Tree Maker should warn you when you enter unlikely dates (for example a death date that occurs earlier than the individual's birth date).

Spell Check

Specify how Family Tree Maker's spell check should work, specifically what words it should ignore. The default setting is to "Ignore known names" and "Ignore words with number." Some people prefer to enter surnames in capital letters to distinguish them from first and middle names. If this is your preference, you will likely want spell check to ignore capitalized words.

Navigation

By default, the Edit Individual dialog box opens when you click on a name in trees and in reports or when you double-click on a name in Pedigree View. You can change the default to open Family View. However, if you do, keep in mind that this guidebook assumes that when you double-click on a name, you will open the Edit Individual dialog box, not Family View.

Use Fastfields for

Fastfields speed up data entry by automatically filling in repetitive data as you type in the Family View fields and elsewhere. For example, if you type "San Jose, California" into a location field, then go to another location field and begin to type "San," Family Tree Maker will recognize the similarity and suggest "San Jose, California." By default, all Fastfield options are checked, but you may uncheck any that you wish to turn off. Fastfields are discussed in Chapter 1.

Edit Individual/Marriage Fact Columns

Family Tree Maker will automatically adjust the width of the columns in the Edit Individual and Edit Marriage dialog boxes for you. Leave this box unchecked if you would rather adjust the columns yourself by placing your mouse on a column and dragging it to the desired size.

Dates Tab

Click on the Dates tab in the Preferences dialog box. The Dates tab covers five main areas: Date display format, Date input format, Double Dates, Date labels, and Range styles. If you do not like the selections you make, you can always reset your preferences to Family Tree Maker's default settings by pressing the **Use Defaults** button in the right-hand column. Preference selections for dates include radio buttons, drop-down lists, and fields in which you can type specific changes.

Date Display Format

• **Order** – Click the **MDY** radio button if you want the month to appear before the day (e.g., January 07, 1995). Click the **DMY** radio button if you want the day to appear before the month (e.g., 07 January 1995). By default, Family Tree Maker displays dates in the accepted genealogical date standard, DMY.

•**Styles** – Click the drop-down lists and make selections for the month, day, and year formats, e.g., 5 Mar 2004 vs. 05 March 2004.

Date Input Format

• **MDY or DMY** – Click to select how you want Family Tree Maker to interpret the information you input for dates, in Month Day Year order or Day Month Year order.

Double Dates

• **Cutoff year** – Change the year in this field to change the default double date cutoff year. If you do not want double dates to print, set the double date cutoff year to zero.

> **NOTE**
>
> Calendars changed systems in 1752, moving from Julian to Gregorian. In the Julian system, the first day of the year was March 25. In today's Gregorian system, January 1 is the first day of the year. A date that falls between January and March before 1752 can be interpreted in two ways, and some genealogists prefer to show both dates. For example, February 22 could fall in the year 1750 according to the Gregorian calendar, so the date would be noted as 22 February 1750/51. You can set the year at which you wish to display both date interpretations.

> **NOTE**
>
> This setting applies only to the Family File you have open and will not carry over into other files. The default setting is 0, but if you open a file that already has a cut-off year selected, Family Tree Maker will retain that setting in that particular file.

Date labels

• **About** – If you want Family Tree Maker to display different text for the term "About" (meaning "Circa") in reports, trees, and other views, enter your preferred label in the field indicated.

• **Abt** – If you want Family Tree Maker to display a different abbreviation for the term "Abt" in reports, trees, and other views, enter your preferred label in the field indicated.

> **NOTE**
>
> When entering dates/location information, if you change the preference for this item, it will only apply to the window from which you opened the Preferences dialog box and any window in which you enter dates from this point. Dates which have already been entered using a different date label, e.g., using Abt instead of Ca, will remain unchanged.

> **NOTE**
>
> This setting applies only to the Family File you have open and will not carry over into other files.

Range Styles

• **Prefix** — Click the drop-down lists and make a selection for the date range prefix (Bet., Btn., or blank).

• **Separator** — Click the drop-down lists and make a selection for the date range separator (-, to, and, or &).

> **NOTE**
>
> If you change the preference for Prefix or Separator, the change will apply only to the current Family File. You will need to make this selection again for other Family Files you create or have created.

Labels, Titles, LDS tab

The Labels, Titles, LDS tab allows you to change how fields in the program are labeled. These are fairly standard labels that you will not likely need to change. However, if you do want to change a label, click in the field, highlight the word, and type a new word over the previous label word.

> **NOTE**
>
> If you change the preference for any item in the Labels, Titles, LDS tab, it will apply only to the current Family File. You will need to make this selection again for other Family Files you create or have created.

• **Titles** – Enter titles to use for married and unmarried males, females, and children if you do not like the default titles. Also select the age at which an individual should be assigned an "adult" title, such as "Mr."

• **Labels** – Enter labels that will be used to refer to basic family relationships. For example, you can change Husband and Wife to Father and Mother or Spouse 1 and Spouse 2.

• **Add LDS formats to reports and use LDS layout for family group sheets** – Click this checkbox to add the following report formats of particular interest to members of The Church of Latter-day Saints (LDS church). These appear in the Report Format dialog box in most Reports views:

– LDS: Incomplete Individual Ordinances

– LDS: Incomplete Marriage Sealings

Also note that if you select the LDS checkbox, the labels for Husband, Wife, Marriage, and Married revert to defaults. The Family Group Sheet will also change. In addition, you can use special LDS Ordinance codes even if you do not select this preference.

• **Use Defaults button** – Click the **Use Defaults** button to return the preferences to the original Family Tree Maker defaults.

Images Tab

Click on the **Images tab** of the Preferences dialog box to view the preferences available in the Images tab. Family Tree Maker has established default quality settings for images imported into your scrapbook. While the defaults are usually suitable, there are times when you may want to see what changing the settings does to the quality of the output. You can only make changes while importing the original file, so you will need to access the original image and import it again.

Compression

Click the radio button corresponding to the degree of compression that you want for your picture. Higher ratios give you a greater loss in picture quality, but the pictures will take up less space on your hard disk. Lower ratios give you pictures with less quality loss, but will take up more disk space.

Photo CD Resolution

Click the resolution radio button next to the size you would like your photo CD pictures to be when you add them to the scrapbook. In general, a higher resolution will present a clearer picture. However, the higher the resolution the larger the file size, and the more of your hard disk space the picture will use.

> **NOTE**
>
> These settings apply only to the Family File you have open and will not carry over into other files.

PDF Image Compression

Click the radio button next to the compression quality you would like. The radio buttons allow users of Windows 98 and ME to improve print quality, which can suffer when images have been resized and then converted to PDF format. (This problem may affect certain Family Tree Templates, such as USA Flag and New World.) When checked, this option improves picture quality, but it also results in very large PDF output files. You may want to experiment with the compression to see how it changes the picture. Print a single picture using different compression options. Remember that the less compression used the larger the picture file will be on your computer.

> **NOTE**
>
> This setting applies only to the Family File you have open and will not carry over into other files.

Reference Numbers Tab

Some researchers prefer to use reference numbers for each individual to coincide with their pedigree chart numbers or filing system. At one time, genealogy programs relied on these numbers to find someone in the database. Today's software uses names; Family Tree Maker searches for individuals using the Index of Individuals dialog box or the bookmark or history features. You can also add reference numbers for marriages by clicking in the marriages check box.

This preference setting will cause Family Tree Maker to automatically assign reference numbers, but you can also type in your own reference number for each individual in the Edit Individual dialog box, under the Options tab.

To save reference numbers to your Family File:

1. Click on **Reference Numbers**. The Reference Numbers options will be brought to the front of the Preferences dialog box.

2. Click on the **Individuals** check box. The Individuals reference number will be activated.

3. Click on the **appropriate** number option. The reference numbers will adhere to the selection made.

NOTE

Once the reference number options have been selected, you will need to remember to turn on the display options in the appropriate reports to view the numbers.

4. Click on **OK**. The Preferences dialog box will close and the changes made will take effect.

NOTE

After you have turned on this preference option, you can view the reference number for each individual by opening the individual's Edit Individual dialog box and clicking the Options tab or by opening the Edit Marriage dialog box and clicking the General tab.

Using Family Tree Maker Tools

While researching and entering information about your family, you may need to figure out how individuals are related or to calculate the approximate birth year of an individual. You may want to check how many individuals or generations you have entered in your Family File. Family Tree Make offers calculators and other tools to assist you with these functions and more. In this chapter, you'll learn how to:

- Use relationship, Soundex, and date calculators

- View general statistics about your Family File

- Compact your Family File

Family Tree Maker has special tools to help you figure out dates and how people are related. You might know your great-grandfather's estimated age when he died and the year he died. Use the date calculator to figure out an approximate year of birth so you can look for him in the U.S. census. You can also view statistics about the number of names added to your Family File, who compiled the Family File, and more.

Using Relationship, Soundex, and Date Calculators

Family Tree Maker has three calculators to assist you with relationships between individuals, names, and estimated dates and ages.

To access these calculators:

1. Click on the **Tools** menu.

2. Click the **Relationship Calculator**, **Soundex Calculator**, or the **Date Calculator**. The appropriate calculator will open in a dialog box.

Relationship Calculator

The Relationship Calculator automatically calculates the relationship for any two individuals in your Family File. It also gives you their canon and civil numbers, and in some cases, will identify their nearest common relative.

1. Click **Relationship Calculator** from the **Tools** menu. There will already be two names in the Relationship Calculator dialog box based on the names you are currently viewing in your Family File.

2. Click **Calculate**. The box below the Calculate button will make a statement about the relationship between two individuals.

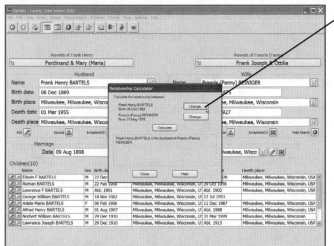

3. Click the upper **Change** button. The Index of Individual dialog box will open.

4. Click the name of one of two individuals whose relationship you would like to compare.

5. Click **OK**.

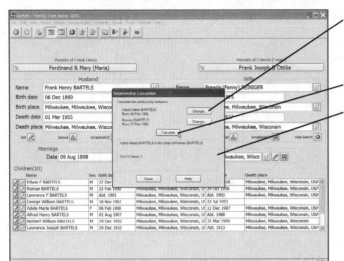

6. Click the lower **Change** button and follow Step 4 again for the second individual.

7. Click **Calculate**.

8. The box below the Calculate button will make a new statement about the relationship between the two new individuals you have selected.

Soundex Calculator

Soundex is a familiar term to genealogists. The Soundex method is a coding system that was used by the government to create indices of the U.S. census records based on how the surname sounds rather than how the surname is spelled. This was done in order to accommodate potential spelling errors. For example, "Smith" may be spelled "Smythe," "Smithe" and "Smythe." The Soundex index was created by coding surnames on their consonant sounds rather than their spelling. By Soundex, the Smith examples given all sound the same, so they would be identified by the same Soundex code (S530). Family Tree Maker can automatically determine the Soundex code for any name, which can be used to find microfilms of certain census returns.

To use the Soundex calculator:

1. Click **Soundex Calculator** from the **Tools** menu. The Soundex Calculator dialog box will open.

2. Type a surname into the **Name** field or click **Choose** to select a name from the Index of Individual dialog box. The Soundex value automatically changes as you enter the information into the field.

3. Click **Close** to exit the Soundex calculator.

Date Calculator

Use the Date calculator to calculate an individuals' birth date, an individual's age at the time of an event, or the date of an event. You need to know two of these items to calculate the third. Try this sample date calculation.

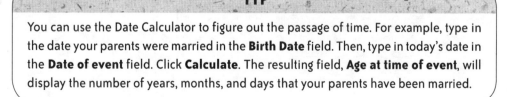

1. Click **Date Calculator** from the **Tools** menu.

2. Click in the **Date of Event** field and type "December 25, 2000." The date will automatically change to standard genealogy format.

3. Type your birth date into the **Birth date** field.

4. Click **Calculate**. The remaining field, **Age at time of event**, will be filled in. You now know your age on December 25, 2000.

Try another calculation. If you know the date an ancestor was married and their approximate age, you can fill that in, then click **Calculate**. Since the birth date field may still be populated from your last entry, Family Tree Maker will ask you to clarify which detail you want calculated. Click **Birth Date**. The Birth Date will be calculated.

TIP

You can use the Date Calculator to figure out the passage of time. For example, type in the date your parents were married in the **Birth Date** field. Then, type in today's date in the **Date of event** field. Click **Calculate**. The resulting field, **Age at time of event**, will display the number of years, months, and days that your parents have been married.

Viewing General Statistics on Your Family File

You can learn some general statistics about the size of your Family File and more.

1. Click **Family File Statistics** from the **Tools** menu. The statistics will appear automatically in the Family File Statistics dialog box, except for the total number of generations and total number of different surnames.

2. Click **calculate** next to **Generations** and **Surnames** to calculate those figures.

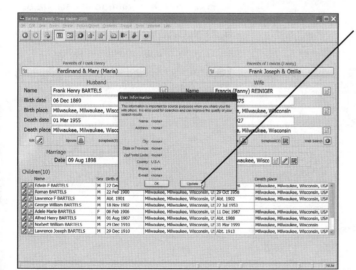

You can add information about or view who created a Family File.

1. Click **User Information** from the **Tools** menu. The User Information dialog box will open. If you are viewing someone else's family file, the details of this page may be filled in.

2. Click **Update** if you are viewing your own family file. Family Tree Maker will ask you if you are related to the individuals in the file.

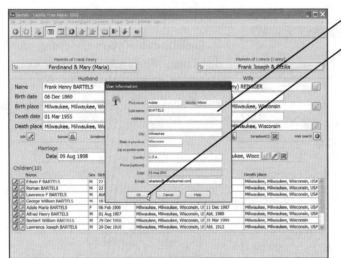

3. If you are related:

a. Click **Yes**. Family Tree Maker will ask you to select yourself in the Index of Individuals file. Click **OK**.

b. Click your name from the Index of Individuals dialog box and click **OK**. The User Information fill-in sheet will open.

If you are not related:

c. Click **No**. The User Information fill-in sheet will open.

4. Enter your information in each field.

5. Click **OK**. The dialog box will close and the information will be saved to your Family File.

Compacting Your Family File

Family Tree Maker contains a database in which you may delete a lot of data. However, even though the data has been removed from the file, the file may still remain at a larger size. You should compact your file periodically to optimize the Family File, remove unnecessary items, and re-index the file to make it more efficient. This process may also find and correct problems with your file.

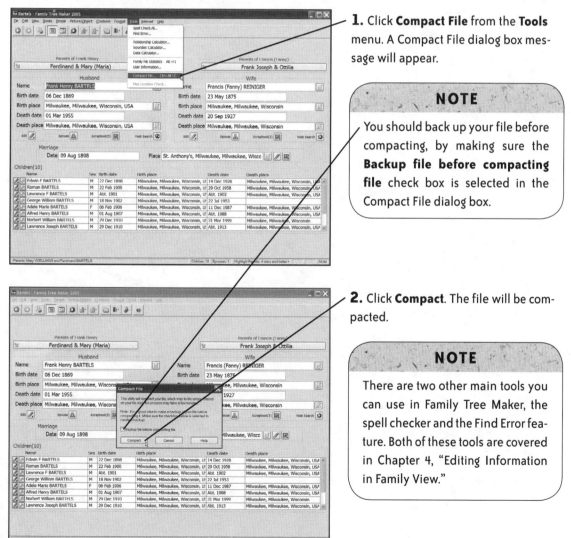

1. Click **Compact File** from the **Tools** menu. A Compact File dialog box message will appear.

NOTE

You should back up your file before compacting, by making sure the **Backup file before compacting file** check box is selected in the Compact File dialog box.

2. Click **Compact**. The file will be compacted.

NOTE

There are two other main tools you can use in Family Tree Maker, the spell checker and the Find Error feature. Both of these tools are covered in Chapter 4, "Editing Information in Family View."

PART

VII

Appendixes

A

Installing Family Tree Maker 2005

Family Tree Maker has been designed to be easy to install. In this first appendix, you will learn how to:

- Install Family Tree Maker on your computer
- Choose components you want to install
- Uninstall Family Tree Maker

Most computers use an auto-run feature when you put a new program CD into your CD-ROM drive—the CD begins to run without your having to do anything.

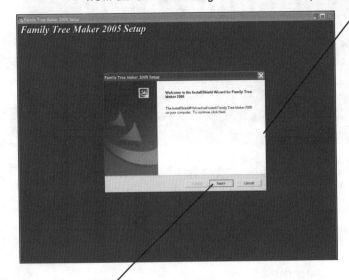

1. Insert the Family Tree Maker 2005 CD into your computer's CD-ROM drive. The automatic installer will start. You will be viewing the Family Tree Maker 2005 Setup dialog box with the welcome wizard.

> **NOTE**
>
> Family Tree Maker will encourage you to close any programs you have running at the time you begin to install Family Tree Maker 2005. This is recommended whenever you install new software.

2. Click **Next**. The Access Your Online Data dialog box will appear. Read the message.

3. Click **Next**. The License Agreement will appear. Read the message, using the scroll bar on the right to navigate to the end.

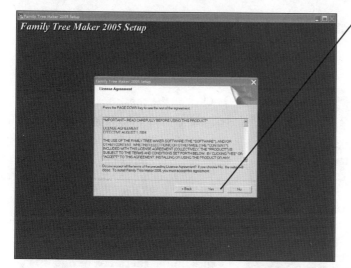

4. Click **Yes** after you read the message. The Choose Destination Location dialog box will appear. Family Tree Maker will automatically select a location to save your program.

5. Click **Next** if you approve of the location Family Tree Maker has chosen (recommended) or click **Browse** to choose your own location. The Components dialog page will appear.

Choosing Components

Family Tree Maker allows you to decide which of the available components you want to install.

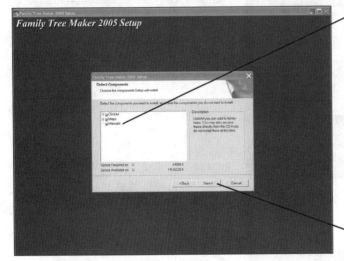

1. Click on the check box next to the component you want to install.

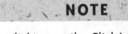

> **NOTE**
>
> By clicking on the ClickArt or Maps check box you automatically select all of the indented items under each heading. To exclude an item, click on the check box next to it to remove the checkmark.

2. Click on **Next**. The Select Components dialog box will close and Family Tree Maker will begin to install. After the initial installation is completed, you will be asked to select your Internet Connectivity Options.

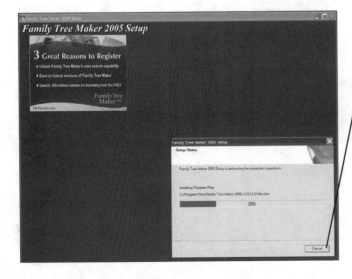

> **NOTE**
>
> You can cancel the installation while it is in progress by clicking **Cancel**.

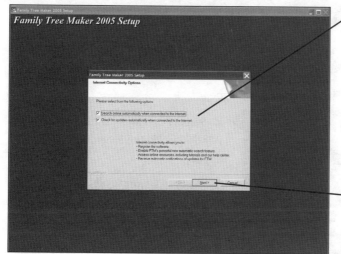

3. Click in each checkbox to remove the check mark if you do not want to automatically search online when connected to the Internet and if you do not want to automatically search for updates when connected to the Internet. You can change these settings later from within the program, but this setting is recommended.

4. Click **Next** to save your selections. You will be taken to the InstallShield Wizard Complete page.

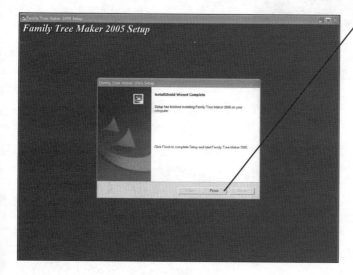

5. Click **Finish**. The installation page will close.

Uninstalling Family Tree Maker

There might come a time when you need to remove Family Tree Maker from your computer. Family Tree Maker has included an uninstall option.

1. Click on the **Start** button. The Start menu will appear.

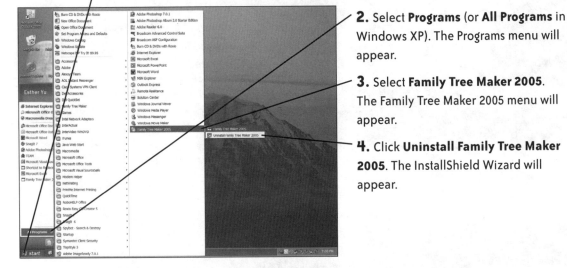

2. Select **Programs** (or **All Programs** in Windows XP). The Programs menu will appear.

3. Select **Family Tree Maker 2005**. The Family Tree Maker 2005 menu will appear.

4. Click **Uninstall Family Tree Maker 2005**. The InstallShield Wizard will appear.

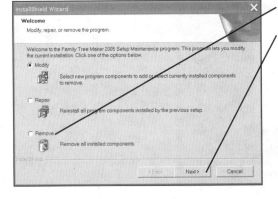

5. Click on the **Remove** radio button.

6. Click on **Next**. The InstallShield will verify you want to remove the program. Clicking **No** will cancel the operation.

> ### NOTE
>
> On occasion you may find it necessary to reinstall the program if you are having problems. To do this make sure to select the radio button next to Repair. When you wish to add clip art or maps that you did not install originally, select the Modify option.

B Using Keyboard Shortcuts

Many people prefer not to have to reach for the mouse when they are entering information. Keyboard shortcuts allow you to perform many tasks on the keyboard instead of with the mouse. Throughout the book, your attention has been called to some of the keyboard shortcuts included in this appendix, but here you can see the information at a glance. In this appendix, you'll learn how to:

- Use the keyboard shortcuts in Family Tree Maker

- Use keyboard combinations in text windows

Learning Keyboard Shortcuts

As you spend more time with Family Tree Maker, you will find these shortcut keys especially useful.

Don't forget, you learned in Chapter 2 how to find shortcuts for most functions in Family Tree Maker. This is simply a table of the most commonly used shortcuts.

Getting Help

Although you can always open the Help menu, you can use the keyboard shortcuts shown in the following table to get to the help you need more quickly.

To execute this command	Do this
View Help for the Current Page	Press the F1 key
Use the What's This Button	Press the Shift and F1 keys at the same time (Shift+F1)

Working in Family Tree Maker

The following table puts the keyboard shortcuts related to Family Tree Maker commands together for an easy reference.

To execute this command	Do this
Create a new Family File	Press Ctrl+N
Open a different Family File	Press Ctrl+O
Print a report	Press Ctrl+P
Undo/Redo	Press Ctrl+Z
Create a new To-Do item	Press Ctrl+T
Access the Index of Individuals	Press F2
View a source	Press Ctrl+S
Open the Other Spouses dialog box	Press F3
Add bookmark	Press Ctrl+B

To execute this command	Do this
More about Picture/Object dialog box	Press Ctrl+M
Compact File	Press Ctrl+Alt+C
Get Family File status	Press Alt+F1
Get system information	Press Ctrl+F1
Exit Family Tree Maker 2005	Press Alt+F4

Working with Text

While most of the entries in Family Tree Maker are made in fields, there are a number of text windows for typing notes. The following tables contain some shortcuts you might find useful when working in the text windows.

Selecting Text

The first step in manipulating your text is to select it. The following table offers some keyboard combinations for selecting a letter, a word, a line, or more.

To execute this command	Do this
Highlight the character to the right of the insertion point	Press Shift+Right Arrow
Highlight the character to the left of the insertion point	Press Shift+Left Arrow
Highlight an entire word to the right of the insertion point	Press Ctrl+Shift+Right Arrow
Highlight an entire word to the left of the insertion point	Press Ctrl+Shift+Left Arrow
Highlight an entire line	Press Shift+End
Highlight a paragraph one line at a time	Press Shift+Down Arrow for each line of the paragraph
Highlight all lines above the insertion point	Press Ctrl+Shift+Home

Copying and Pasting Text and Records of Individuals

After you select the text or individual(s) you want to work with, you might want to remove it or copy it for placement elsewhere. The following table contains the keyboard combinations you need to manipulate selected text or information about individuals.

To execute this command	Do this
Copy text	Press Ctrl+C
Cut text	Press Ctrl+X
Paste text	Press Ctrl+V
Delete text	Press Del
Copy Selected Individual	Press Ctrl+I
Copy All individuals in Family Page	Press Ctrl+A

Glossary

Ahnentafel. German for *ancestor table*. In addition to being a chart, it also refers to a genealogical numbering system.

Ancestor. A person from whom one descends.

Ancestor Tree. Also known as a *Pedigree Chart,* this chart begins with a specific individual and displays direct lineage of all of the individual's ancestors.

Annotation. Personal notes or comments that either explain or critique. Family Tree Maker employs annotations in the Bibliography Report.

Bibliography. A report that shows a list of sources used to compile the information included in the genealogy. The sources follow an accepted format, which Family Tree Maker has built into the program.

BMP. Bitmap. A file format for graphics.

Book. In Family Tree Maker, a compilation of reports generated for a family or an individual, including family trees, miscellaneous reports, stories, photos, a table of contents, and an index.

Brightness. An adjustment that can be made to scanned images to make the image lighter or darker.

Browser. See *Web browser*.

Case Sensitive. Differentiating between uppercase and lowercase characters.

Citation. The accepted notation of the source of information.

Cite. The act of making note of the proof that supports a conclusion or claimed fact in the genealogy.

Click. The action of pressing and releasing a mouse button. Usually, when a program instructs you to click on an item, it is referring to the left side of the mouse. A program may specify "left-click" or "right-click." You can also double-click by pressing and releasing the mouse button twice in rapid succession.

Clipboard. A memory feature of the Windows environment that allows a person to copy or cut text or graphics from one document and paste them into another.

Contrast. An adjustment made to scanned images that causes the image to brighten or dim.

Compression. A setting that determines the quality of the images and the size of the image files you are working with in Family Tree Maker that will be put in your scrapbook and printed out on trees and reports.

CSV. Comma Separated Value(s). A file that separates data by comma which then allows importing into a spreadsheet program.

Cue Cards. The pop-up help windows that appear when you move from screen to screen in Family Tree Maker. They can be turned on or off using the system preferences.

Descendant. A person who descends lineally from another.

Descendant Tree. A chart that lists an individual and his or her descendants.

Dialog Box. Small windows that display on your screen and help you carry out different tasks for the program. Generally, dialog boxes contain command buttons and various options to help you carry out a command or task.

Endnotes. Source citations and explanatory notes that appear at the end of a document, specifically a tree or report.

Export. To transfer data from one computer to another or from one computer program to another.

Family File. Family Tree Maker's name for the database that contains the information about your lineage, e.g., you could create a Family File for Smith family and Jones family.

FamilyFinder Index. A genealogical list containing over 750 million names that is included in Family Tree Maker's CDs and online at Genealogy.com.

Family Group Sheet. A form that displays information on a single, complete family unit.

Family View. The main screen in Family Tree Maker, into which you enter information about a particular individual and family.

File Format. The file format in which you save a document indicates what program will open the file. Each file can only be opened by certain programs. The file formats are automatically attached to the end of a file name, but you can change the file format when you are saving it. Family Tree Makers uses the .FTW extension file format, or, for back-up copies, it uses .FBK.

Fastfields. Family Tree Maker remembers the names of the last 50 locations you have typed in so that as you begin to type in a place in a new location field, Family Tree Maker shows you possible matches based on the letters you have typed up to that point.

Format. One of Family Tree Maker's options for developing the style and look of reports and trees.

GEDCOM. GEnealogical Data COMmunication. A standard designed by the Family History Department of the Church of Jesus Christ of Latter-Day Saints for transferring data between different genealogy software packages.

Genealogy Report. A narrative style report that details a family through one or more generations and includes basic facts about each member in addition to biographical information that was entered through Family Tree Maker.

Generation. The period of time between the birth of one group of individuals and the next--usually about 25 to 33 years.

GIF. Graphic Interchange Format. A graphic file format that is widely used in Web page documents.

Given Name. The first name (and middle name) given to a child at birth or at his or her baptism. Also known as a *Christian name*.

Home Page. The main page of a website.

Hourglass Tree. A chart showing both the ancestors and the descendants of a selected individual. When printed, the tree resembles an hourglass because the ancestors spread out above the selected individual and the descendants spread out below.

HTML. Hypertext Markup Language. The standard language for creating and formatting Web pages.

Icon. A small graphic picture or symbol that represents a program, file, or folder on your computer. Clicking on an icon with a mouse generally causes the program to run, the folder to open, or the file to be displayed. Sometimes, you have to double-click an item instead of just clicking once. (See Click in glossary.)

Import. To bring into a program a file that was created using another program.

Edit Individual Dialog Box. A multi-tabbed dialog box that allows you to easily edit and view information for a specific individual you have recorded in Family Tree Maker.

Edit Marriage Dialog Box. A multi-tabbed dialog box that allows you to easily view and edit personal information about a marriage or similar relationship between two individuals.

Inline Notes. The sources that appear within the text as opposed to at the bottom or end of a page in Family Tree Maker's Genealogy Reports.

Kinship. In genealogy, this refers to the relationship between one individual and any or all of his or her relatives. This can be displayed through the Kinship Report in Family Tree Maker.

JPEG. Joint Photographic Expert Group. Graphics that use the .jpg extension include a compression technique that reduces the size of the graphics file.

Maternal Ancestor. An ancestor on the mother's side of the family.

Merge. The ability in Family Tree Maker to take the information of two individuals who appear to be the same person and combine them into a single individual in the Family File.

NGSQ. *National Genealogical Society Quarterly*. A periodical published by that society. Also refers to the NGS Quarterly numbering system offered in descending genealogy reports.

OLE. Object Linking and Embedding. A technology that allows you to create items in one program and place them in another, including video clips, still images, pictures, word-processing files, and spreadsheet files.

Outline Descendant Tree. A chart that shows in an indented outline format an individual's children, grandchildren, great-grandchildren, and so on through the generations.

Paternal Ancestor. An ancestor on the father's side of the family.

PDF. Portable Document Format. A file format that retains printer formatting so that when it is opened it looks as it would if on the printed page. Requires Adobe Acrobat Reader to open and view a file that ends in the .PDF extension.

Pedigree Chart. A chart that shows the direct ancestors of an individual. Known in Family Tree Maker as an *Ancestor Tree*.

Pedigree View. The second main screen in Family Tree Maker, into which you view the linear relationship between individuals in an interactive pedigree chart.

Preferred. A term Family Tree Maker uses in reference to parents, spouses, or duplicate events, meaning that you want to see that selection first or have it displayed in trees and reports.

Primary or Root Individual. The main individual in any of the Family Tree Maker charts or reports.

Red-Eye Removal. The method of removing the red, or hollow, look of eyes from flash photographs that have been digitized.

Register. Refers to the descending genealogy format used by the New England Historic Genealogical Society. This also refers to their periodical by the same name.

Reports. Any of a number of standard and custom displays in various formats that Family Tree Maker can create.

Research Journal. A record used by genealogists to keep track of their research findings and tasks to be accomplished.

Resolution. In Family Tree Make an option allowed when working with Kodak Photo CD files that allows you to increase the size of a picture thus making it a clearer picture.

Re-Writable CD-ROM. A CD-ROM drive that allows you to save files to a CD-RW disc, a disc designed to be used like a floppy disc and to which you can write to more than once (different from a Writable CD-ROM).

RTF. Rich Text Format. A cross-platform, cross-application text document format. It retains some of the formatting information that is supported by many word processors.

Root or Primary Individual. The main individual in any of the Family Tree Maker charts, reports, or views.

Saturation. The amount of color in each pixel of an image. When the saturation is high, the image shows bright, vivid colors. When the saturation is low, the picture may look black and white.

Scrapbooks. The term used by Family Tree Maker for the collections of photographs, images, video, sound, and OLE objects that can be stored for each individual and marriage in the Family File.

Siblings. Children of the same parents.

Source. The record, such as a book, an e-mail message, or an interview, from which specific information was obtained.

Spouse. The person to whom another person is married.

Surname. The family name or last name of an individual.

Threshold. As used in the Red-Eye Removal Dialog box, the minimum degree of redness for the pixels to be fixed.

Tree. The term Family Tree Maker uses to refer to its various charts. See *Ancestor Tree*, *Descendant Tree*, and *Outline Descendant Tree*.

URL. Uniform Resource Locator. The address used by a Web browser to locate a page on the Web.

User Home Page. The section of Genealogy.com where individual researcher's data is shared on the Web.

WAV. Windows Audio Visual. The sound files that work with Media Player and Sound Recorder.

Web browser. The software that lets you access pages on the Web. The browser reads the HTML code and converts it to the pictures, colors, menu options, and overall design that you view on your monitor.

Web Merge. A Family Tree Maker wizard that allows you to merges Web results you have found on Ancestry.com to your Family File.

Web Search. A Family Tree Maker function that automatically searches Ancestry.com for records containing information about your ancestors.

Web page. A document on the Internet that is written using a scripting language such as HTML.

Website. A location on the Internet maintained by a single individual, company, or entity that provides information, graphics, and other items.

World Family Tree (WFT) Project. A multi-volume CD and online collection created by Genealogy.com from the genealogies submitted electronically by family history enthusiasts and indexed in the FamilyFinder Index.

World Wide Web. A graphical interface that is composed of Internet sites that provide researchers with access to documents and other files.

Writable CD-ROM. A CD-ROM drive that allows you to save files to a CD-R disc, a disc designed to be used like a floppy disc.

Index

A

addresses
    creating Address Reports, 196, 197
    entering, 50, 61
ages, calculating, 333
Ahnentafel format reports, 174, 351
aliases, 10, 34, 52
All-in-One Trees
    adding images, 159–64
    changing the text font, 152, 153
    creating, 144
    customizing borders and backgrounds, 153–56
    pruning the display, 149–51
    saving, 156, 168, 169
    using templates to enhance, 157
    See also Ancestor Trees; Descendant Trees;
        Hourglass Trees; InterneTrees; printing
Alternate Facts Reports, 53, 54, 196
Ancestor Trees
    adding images, 159–64
    changing the text font, 152, 153
    creating a Fan Chart, 144
    creating a Pedigree Chart, 144
    creating a Vertical Ancestor Tree, 144
    customizing borders and backgrounds, 153–56
    formats for displaying information, 146, 147
    including siblings on, 148–49
    rearrange, 147, 148
    saving, 156, 168, 169
    sharing a Standard Pedigree Tree, 144
    using templates to enhance, 157
    See also All-in-One Trees; charts; Descendant
        Trees; Hourglass Trees; InterneTrees; printing

B

backing up files, 80, 294, 311, 312
Bibliography Reports, 116, 177, 178, 351
Birthday Reports, 198, 203, 206
births, entering information about, 9, 10, 35, 53, 54, 75
book. *See* family history books

C

calculating dates, 333
calculating relationships, 330–32
charts
    adding empty branches, 158
    adding images, 159–64, 185
    adding siblings, 148–49, 151
    customizing, 145–59
    formatting, 145–59
    including and excluding items, 62, 149–51
    printing, 164–68
    saving, 168, 169
    templates, 145, 157, 158, 327
    See also All-in-one Trees; Ancestor Trees;
        Descendant Trees; Fan Charts; Hourglass
        Trees; Pedigree Charts
children
    adding, 17, 18, 34
    adding another set of parents, 38–45
    adding siblings, 148–49
    detaching a child from the wrong parents, 71
    linking a child to parents, 70, 71
    moving a child, 79

O

OLE (Object Linking and Embedding) objects, 124–27

P

parents
  adding another set of, 38–40, 45, 46
  detaching a child from the wrong, 71
  linking children to, 43–45, 70–71
  using maiden names, 9, 34
  See also Family View, names
Pedigree Charts, customizing, 146
Pedigree View
  bookmark, 99, 100
  changing the number of generations, 93–94
  changing the root individual, 91–93
  editing, 100–03
  filtering the index, 97, 98
  navigating, 95
  opening, 90
  side panel, 96-100
  Web search in, 94
  See also preferences
photographs
  access a scrapbook, 118
  adding images and other multimedia objects,
    119
  adjusting color and brightness, 133
  attaching image to source, 114, 115
  correcting red eye, 133–35
  inserting in scrapbooks, 204
  See also scrapbooks
place names. *See* entering details
preferences
  accessing, 315
  animation in Pedigree View, 318
  automatic updates on Internet, 317
  backing up files and protecting file names, 316
  changing the look and feel of screens, 317
  color, 317
  dates, 323, 324
  editing, 320, 322

error checking during data entry, 321
  Fastfields, 322
  generations in view, 318
  images, 325, 327
  labels, 324, 325
  Latter-day Saint, 325
  measurements, 318
  navigation, 322
  online, 317
  Pedigree View, 318, 319
  picture quality, 326, 327
  reference numbers, 327
  searching, 318, 319
  source Information, 319
  splash screen, 317
  spell check, 322
  titles, 319
  toolbar, 319, 320
primary individuals, entering, 8, 88, 91, 93, 95
printing
  Family View, 57, 58
  general instructions, 144
  notes, 57, 58
  scrapbook pages, 138–40
  source information, 116
privacy, 274
protecting file names, 316, 317
publishing. *See* family history books; family home
  pages

R

reference numbers, 62, 64, 316, 327, 328
Register format reports, 173
relationships
  calculating, 330–32
  detaching a child from the wrong parents, 71
  linking children to parents, 70, 71
  See also children, spouses
Reports
  formatting, 173–76
  selecting and viewing, 176–82
  See also addresses; Alternate Facts Reports;
    Bibliography Reports; Birthday Reports;
    Custom Reports; Documented Events
    Reports; family history books; family home

U

undo, 77, 85, 158, 227, 258, 311, 348
uninstalling Family Tree Maker, 346

V

Vertical Ancestor Trees, 26, 144, 147, 149, 351
views
    Pedigree View. *See* Pedigree View
    Family View. *See* Family View
    See also charts; reports

W

Web Merge report, 223–28
Web page. *See* family home pages
Web Search report
    automatic search, 216
    filter results, 220–23
    setting a search threshold, 217
    Web Search report, 217–20
    See also preferences
welcome screen, 5–8

About the Author

Esther Yu Sumner has been editing and writing in the genealogy industry for over five years. She has been published in *Ancestry* Magazine and in the *Ancestry Daily News*. In addition, she is a former contributing editor to *Ancestry* Magazine and *Genealogical Computing* and the former associate editor of the *Ancestry Daily News* and the *Ancestry Daily News Collector's Edition* books. She was also a contributing editor to *Celebrating the Family* and Genealogy.com's *Research Spotlight,* and currently edits and writes the *MyFamily Weekly* newsletter. Esther, a California native with a bachelor of arts in print journalism and a minor in English from Brigham Young University, lives in Utah with her husband John.